AS Level for Edexcel

Applied ICT

Series editor:
K. Mary Reid

www.heinemann.co.uk
✓ Free online support
✓ Useful weblinks
✓ 24 hour online ordering

01865 888058

Heinemann Educational Publishers
Halley Court, Jordan Hill, Oxford OX2 8EJ
Part of Harcourt Education

Heinemann is a registered trademark of
Harcourt Education Limited

©Alan Jarvis, Sharon Yull, 2005

First published 2005

10 09 08 07 06 05
10 9 8 7 6 5 4 3 2 1

British Library Cataloguing in Publication Data is available
from the British Library on request.

10-digit ISBN: 0435 462 00 8
13-digit ISBN: 978 0 435462 00 0

Copyright notice
All rights reserved. No part of this publication may be reproduced in any form or by any means (including photocopying or storing it in any medium by electronic means and whether or not transiently or incidentally to some other use of this publication) without the written permission of the copyright owner, except in accordance with the provisions of the Copyright, Designs and Patents Act 1988 or under the terms of a licence issued by the Copyright Licensing Agency, 90 Tottenham Court Road, London W1T 4LP. Applications for the copyright owner's written permission should be addressed to the publisher.

Edited by David Kershaw
Designed by Lorraine Inglis
Typeset by Thomson Digital
Original illustrations © Harcourt Education Limited, 2005
Cover design by Wooden Ark Studios
Printed by Scotprint Ltd
Cover photo: © Photonica

Acknowledgements
Every effort has been made to contact copyright holders of material reproduced in this book. Any omissions will be rectified in subsequent printings if notice is given to the publishers.

Websites
There are links to relevant websites in this book. In order to ensure that the links are up to date, that the links work, and that the sites are not inadvertently linked to sites that could be considered offensive, we have made the links available on the Heinemann website at www.heinemann.co.uk/hotlinks. When you access the site the express code is 2008P.
Please note that the examples of websites suggested in this book were up to date at the time of writing. It is essential for tutors to preview each site before using it to ensure that the URL is still accurate and the content is appropriate. We suggest that tutors bookmark useful sites and consider enabling students to access them through the school or college intranet.

Contents

Acknowledgements — V
Introduction — VI
Standard ways of working — VII

UNIT 1 — The Information age — 1

Introduction — 1
1.1 The information age — 3
1.2 Online services — 12
1.3 Life in the information age — 19
1.4 The digital divide — 23
1.5 What is an e-book? — 26
1.6 Developing an e-book — 29
1.7 ICT skills — 32

UNIT 2 — The Digital Economy — 37

Introduction — 37
2.1 Information needs of organisations — 39
2.2 From 'brick' to 'click' — 43
2.3 Transactional websites — 47
2.4 Back-office processes — 56
2.5 E-customers — 58
2.6 E-consumer awareness — 61
2.7 Security — 63
2.8 The database — 65
2.9 ICT skills — 78

UNIT 3 — The knowledge worker — 81

Introduction — 81
3.1 Problem solving — 83
3.2 The decision-making process — 85
3.3 Understanding the situation — 87
3.4 Sources of information — 88
3.5 Other factors to consider — 94
3.6 Making a decision — 95
3.7 Computer modelling — 97
3.8 Using a model to consider alternatives — 99
3.9 ICT skills — 101

Glossary — 115
Index — 124

Acknowledgements

The authors and publisher would like to thank all those who have granted permission to reproduce copyright material.

Microsoft product screen shots reprinted with permission from Microsoft Corporation.
Pipex screengrab/with permission from PIPEX
Choice Point article by Paul Roberts/TheStandard.com
Bill Gates gets 4 million emails a day/Copyright Guardian Newspapers Limited 2004
Yahoo! Messenger screengrab/Reproduced with permission of Yahoo! Inc. © Yahoo! Inc. and the Yahoo! Logo are trademarks of Yahoo! Inc.
DVLA/Crown copyright material is reproduced with the permission of the Controller of HMSO
P&O Ferries
Interactive online game/Weboggle.shackworks.com
eBay screengrab/eBay
The Digital Divide/BT
flybmi images/Images reproduced with kind permission of bmi

The authors and publisher would like to thank the following for permission to reproduce photographs:

Alamy/page 20
Corbis/page 24
Getty Images/photodisc/page 40
Courtesy of Apple/page 48

Every effort has been made to contact copyright holders of material produced in this book. Any omissions will be rectified in subsequent printings if notice is given to the publishers.

Introduction

This is one in a series of four volumes that covers the Edexcel qualifications in
Applied Information and Communication Technology for GCE. The books are organised like this:

* AS (Single Award), which covers units 1 to 3
* AS (Double Award), which covers units 1 to 6
* A2 (Single Award), which covers units 7, 8, 10, 11, 12
* A2 (Double Award), which covers units 7 to 14.

The two AS Level (Single and Double Award) qualifications are covered by one book each.
The two A Level (Single and Double Award) qualifications are covered by two books each,
one at AS and one at A2 level.

This book covers the three units that are offered in the AS (Single Award):

* Unit 1: The information age
* Unit 2: The digital economy
* Unit 3: The knowledge worker

In addition, 'Standard Ways of Working' runs as a common theme through all the units and
is covered separately. Students are advised to read this before starting on the units.

Assessment

Your achievements on this qualification will be assessed through portfolios of evidence and an
examination. Portfolios will be assessed internally and the examination will be assessed externally.

All the AS units except Unit 3 will be assessed internally. You will be expected to construct an e-portfolio
for each unit. Further guidance on this is given in Standard Ways of Working. Unit 3 will be assessed
externally, through a 2 hour examination. In preparation for the examination you will be given a
scenario to study. The examination itself will be taken at a computer where you will be presented with
additional e-resources, such as a spreadsheet model, to help you solve a problem. Your solution will be
submitted online.

Further information

You can find further information about this qualification at www.edexcel.org.uk. Remember to search
for GCE Applied ICT. You can download the complete specification, which gives full details of all the
units, both AS and A2, and how they are assessed. This document is nearly 300 pages long. Edexcel also
provide a one page Student Guide, which could help you if you are trying to decide whether to study
for this qualification.

A Tutor Resource File will provide additional material for these units.

We hope you enjoy your studies and wish you every success.

K Mary Reid
April 2005

Standard ways of working

Introduction

As an experienced ICT user, you already know a great deal about how to get the best out of your ICT equipment. But you can probably learn some new tricks.

In this chapter you will be comparing the way that you work with the standard ways of working which ICT professionals use. This should help you to act responsibly and legally, to watch out for your own safety, and to save time. Mastering these ways of working will definitely impress a future employer.

File management

There are a number of questions to ask yourself to ensure that you employ standard ways of managing your files. Do you:

* save your work regularly
* use sensible filenames
* organise your files into directories/folders
* make backup copies
* choose appropriate file formats
* limit access to confidential or sensitive files
* use effective virus protection
* use 'readme' files where appropriate to provide technical information e.g. system requirements?

Saving work regularly

It is important to save your work regularly to avoid losing it if your computer crashes. Some people learn this lesson the hard way – as a result of their computer crashing. To avoid it happening:

* save any new file as soon as you start it
* if you can, configure the software to autosave your work at regular intervals.

Using sensible filenames

Which of these is a sensible file name:

* myfile.doc
* janejones.jpg
* Doom.pdf
* Unit 3 Project v1.doc?

Of course, what counts as 'sensible' depends on what you are going to do with the file. At work, you would probably have to pass a file to someone else to use or to read and comment on. The filename should clearly identify:

* what the file contains
* the version number (where appropriate).

Setting up directory/folder structures

You can very quickly build up a large collection of working files, such as word processing documents, databases, spreadsheet workbooks, etc. If you are using Microsoft Windows then these will be normally be placed in the My Documents folder (also known as a directory). You can create as many extra folders as you like within My Documents.

You might think it a good idea to place all your word processing documents in one folder, all your desk top publishing publications in another folder and so on. But many people prefer to organise their work by subject matter instead.

Think about the sorts of activities you will use your computer for, and how you can most usefully organise related files to suit your needs.

When you are working on a networked PC at your centre or at work, then you will only be able to save files in My Documents or possibly in a folder that you share with a group. On a home computer, you will find that you can create folders anywhere you like, and you may want to set up new folders elsewhere on the hard disk system.

Making backups

It is very reassuring to know that your files are backed up. If the system does malfunction then you will be able to retrieve the work that you have spent so much time over.

On a network, the complete system will be backed up at least once a day. This will happen automatically. You might like to ask the network administrator at your centre about the backup procedures that are followed.

On your home computer, you are responsible for making sure that backups are created. You can do this in several ways:

* You can set up some software applications to make a backup of each file as you create it. Whenever you save the file the previously saved version is renamed as the backup copy. Look out for **Options** or **Preferences** in the main menus.

* Copy important files to an external medium such as a CD or external hard disk. You should do this on a regular basis. Important files could include your email address book or key documents that you are working on for assessment.

* Use the Backup utility that is provided with some versions of operating system software.

Choosing appropriate file formats

Did you know that you can save a word processing file in half a dozen different formats?

For example, Figure 1 shows the different options offered in Microsoft Word. If you go to the **File** menu and select **Save As**, you will see all these options under **Save As Type**.

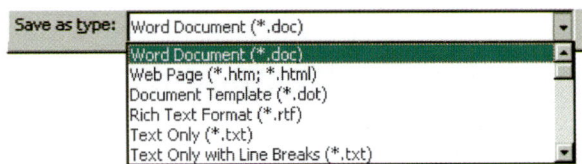

FIGURE 1 *Format options*

The last part of the filename, such as .doc or .txt, indicates which format was used for the file. Do you know what each format can be used for?

* *word document (*.doc)*: a normal word processed document

* *web page (*.htm; *.html)*: for converting into a format suitable for uploading to the web. This is useful for quick conversions of word processed documents for web use, but should not be used for general web design

- *document template (*.doc)*: a document that can be used at any time as a basis for other documents. It will be stored with other templates and available when you create a new page
- *rich text format (*.rtf)*: a simplified word processed format which can be read by many software applications, including older word processing packages. The formatting of the text is preserved, but some of the more specific features, such as footnotes and macros, will be lost
- *text only, and text only with line breaks (*.txt)*: the simplest possible text files, containing ASCII characters, with or without the line break character. These files can be read by any program that handles text.

> **Key term**
>
> ASCII (American Standard Code for Information Interchange) is a set of binary codes that are used to represent text characters in computer systems and communication.

Similarly, images can be saved in a variety of formats including:

- *bitmap (*.bmp)*: stores a colour value for each pixel in the image
- *JPEG (*.jpg)*: a method of compressing bitmaps so they use less memory. This is widely used for photographs and is one of the standard formats used on the World Wide Web
- *graphics interchange format (*.gif)*: another compressed bitmap format used on the Web. It is limited to 256 colour values, so is often used for simple diagrams and icons that do not require finely graduated colour
- *portable network graphics image (*.png)*: a compressed bitmap format that is replacing gifs on the Web
- *tagged image file format (*.tif)*: a widely used bitmap format for storing images on PCs
- *flash movie (*.swf)*: a vector graphic animation format used to develop animations and interactive applications for websites.

There are also a number of specialist formats that are only used by specific graphics applications, as well as audio and video formats. You do need to understand the differences between all these formats, and others, in order to use them effectively.

When you prepare work for publication, you should consider using formats that are 'read only' (i.e. people can access but cannot make changes to). For example, if you allow people to download a word processed file from a website, they will be able to change it without your knowledge. A common 'read only' format is pdf (portable document format) format. You can convert a word processed file into a pdf before you make it available to the general public. You will need to use pdf converter software to do this (e.g. Adobe Acrobat).

Limiting access to confidential or sensitive files

If you want to protect your work from other people you can create a password for it. You may have to read the Help files for your application to find out how to do this.

However, beware of creating password-protected documents if you want to share them with a teacher, assessor or work colleague.

Using effective virus protection

Virus protection is not an optional extra these days. You should refuse to work on any PC that is not adequately protected.

Not only should the right kind of software be installed, but the virus definition files should be updated regularly. In many systems, virus definitions are updated every few hours. This is because new viruses can be transmitted via e-mail to many thousands of computers within minutes.

Networks normally have high levels of virus protection. Check the level of protection that has been installed on the network that you use.

On a home computer, you should download virus protection software if it is not already installed. You will have to pay a modest annual subscription to keep your virus definition files up to date, but this should not be neglected.

Using 'readme' files where appropriate

A ReadMe file contains basic information and advice for a software application. It is supplied as part of the application, ensuring that important information about the application will always be available to the user, even if supporting printed documentation is subsequently lost. It is usually created in a simple text editor, such as Notepad, although you can use a word processing package, then save it in *.txt format.

Personal effectiveness

There are a number of questions to ask yourself to ensure that you employ standard ways of maximising your personal effectiveness. Do you:

* select appropriate ICT tools and techniques
* customise settings in applications
* create and use shortcuts
* use available sources of help
* use a plan to help you organise your work and meet deadlines?

Selecting appropriate ICT tools and techniques

One mark of your effectiveness as a student or employee is whether you use the right tools for the job. For example, you may be asked to produce a simple name and address list for an organisation. You can create this in a word processing package, a spreadsheet or in a database. To decide which to use you need to be able to ask relevant questions, do you want to:

* be able to print out mailing labels
* sort the addresses in different ways
* search the data
* mailmerge the data with letters
* add other types of data?

You will use the answers to such questions to help you determine the ICT tools and techniques appropriate to the task at hand.

Customising settings in applications

It is always helpful and more efficient if you customise the software applications and operating system to match your own needs and preferences.

Some examples include:

* create your own document templates, e.g. to standardise the appearance of your documents
* create macros for commonly performed tasks, so that you can click a single button or combination of keystrokes instead of a series of clicks to perform the same command
* add and remove menu items from the standard toolbars, and create your own toolbars.

Most applications have menu items called **Options**, **Customise** or **Preferences**. Look at these to see the possibilities for customising the settings on your computer to suit your needs better.

Creating and using shortcuts

A shortcut can be placed on your desktop or in a menu. It helps you to go straight to a file, a folder or an application that you use frequently, instead of having to drill down through layers of folders.

In Windows, you can create a shortcut to almost anything by right-clicking on its icon and selecting **Create Shortcut**. The shortcut will be placed in the same folder as the original. You can then move the shortcut to where you want it to go. You can place a shortcut in any of these locations:

* on the desktop
* in the **Start** menu or one of its submenus
* in any folder on your computer.

If you delete a shortcut it does not delete the original file or application.

Using available sources of help

A smart employee does not know everything, but does know where to find things out. This is particularly true of ICT skills. Most people only use about 10 per cent of the facilities in a software application, but when they do need to use a new feature they learn how to use it through the Help resources.

You probably use some sources of help, but you may not be aware of all that are available. Some sources are listed below:

* the CD used to install the software often contains a manual. This is meant to replace, or add to, a printed manual
* the Help menu in software applications may direct you towards:
  – tutorials
  – an index of help topics
  – an answer tool – this may be in the form of a guide like the Office Assistant
  – resources on the Web
* you should be able to find an online community, or other helpful websites, dedicated to getting the most out of your chosen software. Type the software name in your usual search engine.

Using a plan

When you begin a piece of work, you should always decide when you are going to finish it. You may be set a deadline by your employer or teacher, but you would be wise to aim to finish before the deadline. Because life can sometimes get in the way of the best plans (e.g. falling sick, 'losing' work time due to unexpected events, etc.), it is a good idea to build in some buffer time, so that despite the unexpected, you can still meet the deadline.

If it is a substantial project that will take many days or weeks, you can work backwards from the deadline to decide what you need to achieve at key dates. Draw this up as a plan at the beginning, and monitor your progress during the project against the plan. The earlier you establish you are falling behind, the easier it will be to make up the time, or change the plan accordingly.

You may need to provide several different types of documents and files. Again, list what you need to do and fit them into the plan. If you do all this at the beginning you will not be in danger of getting to the end and finding that key components are missing.

Quality assurance

There are a number of questions to ask yourself to ensure that you employ standard ways of assuring the quality of your work. Do you:

* use spell check
* use grammar check
* use print preview
* proofread
* seek the views of others
* authenticate your work?

Using spell check

Unless your spelling and typing skills are perfect, you should always check your spelling in a text document. The spell check can usually be configured through **Options** or **Preferences**, as in the Microsoft Office example in Figure 2.

You can choose to have your spelling checked as you enter it. The software will highlight the incorrect word in some way; if you right-click on the word you will be given a list of alternative spellings to choose from. For example, if you mean to type 'thorough' but accidentally type 'torough' you are offered these alternative spellings: 'thorough', 'trough', 'through', and others. If you are unsure of the correct spelling for the word you want to use, you may need to look up the alternative spellings in a traditional

FIGURE 2 *Configuring spell check preferences*

dictionary to find one which means the same as the one you want to use.

You can also choose to have the spellings of words corrected automatically. To do this, the spell checker draws on its huge bank of regular words. But you need to read your work carefully afterwards, because sometimes the software will 'autocorrect' a word incorrectly and your text may not make sense.

Make sure that the software is using a dictionary that is set for your language. Many software applications are pre-set for US English, and you will probably want to change this to UK English, as spellings do differ, e.g. whether words end in -ise or -ize, or -our or -or (the first in each pair being UK, the second being US spelling).

Using grammar check

The grammar check is another very useful tool, but again can produce very odd results if you do not use it intelligently and carefully check your text at the end.

It is useful to have this set up so that it checks your grammar as you write. It will then highlight errors and offer you alternatives when you right-click. Always read the corrected sentence again to yourself and ask whether it still means what you intended.

Some applications let you select the style of writing that you wish to use, e.g. formal, technical or casual.

Using print preview

You have probably wasted several sheets of paper and considerable time by printing a document before checking what it looks like, only to discover that things don't look right on the printed pages. To avoid this, go to the **File** menu and select **Print Preview** first.

Most applications allow you to change the layout, such as moving margins, in Print Preview mode. This is useful, because you can see the effect on a complete page as you make the changes.

Proofreading

Everyone makes errors when they create documents, and some of these are not detected by spell and grammar checks. Examples include:

* getting your facts wrong
* explaining things in a confusing way
* mistyping names of people and places
* writing ideas in the wrong order
* omitting sentences or paragraphs as you type, or putting them in the wrong places.

These errors can only be identified and corrected by humans, not computers.

The process of reading what you have written very carefully is known as proofreading. If a document is going to be published, like a book or leaflet, then at least two people should proofread it – the author and a second person (whose judgement can be trusted). It is very easy for the original author to overlook errors they have made, but someone else will read it with a fresh eye. Having your material read by an independent eye will not guarantee it will be error-free, but it should help.

A book, such as this one, is checked by a professional proofreader who marks up errors on the printout. These errors are corrected and then checked on subsequent sets of proofs until, ideally, the work is error-free.

Seeking views of others

Colleagues at work and fellow students can all help you to improve your documents. If you ask them to look over your work, then be prepared to do the same for them at some time. You can ask others to:

* proofread your document
* comment on the style and readability
* comment on the design and layout
* comment on the contents
* work with you to improve your work.

You need to be careful asking others to be involved with any of these aspects if the material they are looking at is to be presented as your own work. See the section on plagiarism below. If you are in any doubt about the type of help you can have, then check with your teacher or employer.

Authenticate work

On any document you should always supply, as a header/footer or at some appropriate point in the text, the following information:

* your name
* any other essential details about you, e.g. your department at work or your centre number
* the date on which you completed this version of the document.

These features identify you as the author of the document.

For assessment purposes you will have to produce further evidence to authenticate the work. This can be in the form of a monitoring checklist kept by a teacher, or witness statements. You will also be required to sign a statement that you have completed the work yourself.

Legislation and codes of practice

There are a number of questions to ask yourself to ensure that you conform to the requirements of legislation and codes of practice. Do you:

* acknowledge your sources
* respect copyright
* avoid plagiarism
* protect confidentiality?

Acknowledging sources

If you use or refer to work that someone else has done, then it is only fair to mention them. In fact, in certain circumstances, you could be breaking the law if you do not do so. There are several ways in which you can acknowledge a source:

* use a direct quote, in quotation marks, e.g.

    'Be nice to nerds. Chances are you'll end up working for one.' Bill Gates: *Business @ The Speed of Thought*

* refer to it in the text, e.g.

    Bill Gates once wrote in his book *Business @ The Speed of Thought* that you should be nice to nerds. He said that the chances are you'll end up working for one.

* use a footnote or endnote, e.g.

    It has been said that you should be nice to nerds, because the chances are you'll end up working for one.[14]

At the bottom of the page, or at end of the document, you will see this:

[14] Bill Gates, *Business @ The Speed of Thought*

What you should not do is to write something like this, without acknowledging that Bill Gates originally wrote it:

I think you should be nice to nerds. After all, the chances are you'll end up working for one.

Respect copyright

You will learn about the laws on copyright in detail in Unit 1. If someone writes anything, develops software, designs an image or creates an art object, they have the copyright for that item. That means that only they have the right to copy the material, unless they have given permission to someone else to do so. Copyright lasts throughout the author's lifetime, and for 70 years afterwards (when it is handled by the person's executors).

You can usually use quotes (as we did above) from an item that is under copyright, or use extracts, for educational purposes. The copyright laws are one reason for always acknowledging sources. (If you inadvertently infringe a copyright law but have acknowledged your source(s), it will imply 'good faith' on your part.) Wholesale copying of material, especially when it is then sold by the copier, is illegal. This is often known as piracy, especially in relation to software.

Avoiding plagiarism

Plagiarism occurs when someone passes off someone else's work as his or her own. It can happen in novels, in songwriting and in academic work. The most serious form of plagiarism is when students submit coursework as their own, although it has been written by someone else. Examination boards and universities disqualify students who are found doing this. In some cases the student copies coursework that has been previously submitted successfully; in other cases the student asks someone to write the coursework for them.

You should, of course, not submit work under false pretences. You should also protect your own good work to make sure that noone else tries to pass it off as their own.

One difficulty that some students have is in deciding how much help they should ask for with their work. The best advice is to discuss this with the teacher, who will know exactly how much support they and other people can give you.

Protecting confidentiality

It is good practice not to use the names of living people in anything you write, unless you have their permission. For example, if you are asked, as a student, to write a report on the IT systems within an organisation, you should explain to the member of staff what you are writing and ask permission to refer to them. You may like to send them a copy before you submit it.

If you have data about the customers or clients of an organisation, and you need to refer to them, then it is usual to 'anonymise' their names, addresses and any other identifying information. You can do this either by removing the data altogether, for example, by obscuring any handwritten information (perhaps by using a 'white out' of some sort, or a heavy felt pen). Alternatively, you can use pseudonyms instead of real names, in which case you should mention that you have done so (e.g. writing at the end of the piece of work, 'Names have been changed to protect confidentiality.').

If you are working for an employer and your report is for internal use only, then it is acceptable to use real names in many instances.

You will learn more about the laws that govern information about people in Unit 2.

Safe working

There are a number of questions to ask yourself to ensure that you employ standard ways of working safely. Do you:

* ensure that hardware, cables, seating, etc. are positioned correctly
* ensure that lighting is appropriate
* take regular breaks
* handle and store media correctly?

Ensuring that hardware, cables, seating etc. are positioned correctly

You probably expect to use a computer regularly over many years both for your studies and for work. You need to protect yourself from the risks of accidents or long-term health problems. You will learn about Health and Safety regulations in Unit 1, but most aspects of health and safety are commonsense. Here are some questions to ask about all the PCs you use regularly, whether at your place of study, at home, at work or at a library:

* Are the cables fastened out of reach, so I can't trip on them or pull them accidentally?
* Is the desk the correct height? (When seated, your desk is at the right height if your elbows make an angle of 90° (or slightly greater when you reach the keyboard.) Are the feet planted horizontally on the floor? Is there a footrest if it is too high? (Old telephone directories make a cheap footrest.)
* Can I adjust the seat to view the monitor comfortably? Have I done so? (You should be looking horizontally at or slightly down to the screen.) Does the seat provide appropriate back support? (When you are seated your knees should be at 90°, and the angle between your back and thighs should also be around 90°.)
* Am I at a distance from the screen so I can read it comfortably?

Ensuring that lighting is appropriate

Employers are required to install suitable lighting in rooms where computers are used. The lights should be strong enough and should not flicker. You should also avoid glare on the screens by positioning them so that they do not catch bright sunlight or badly placed desk lights.

You should check the lighting at your place of study and in any room where you use a PC at home. You can also adjust the brightness and contrast on your screen so that it is comfortable to use.

Your eyesight is precious, so do not risk damaging it by using a computer in poor light.

Taking regular breaks

Most computer users are tempted to miss breaks and carry on working for several hours, especially when they are absorbed in an activity. You should aim to take a brief break every hour or so. For five minutes or so get up, walk around, have a drink, do another task. Your eyes will benefit from focusing on something other than the screen, and your work on the computer will actually be more productive as a result of the few minutes break.

Handling and storing media correctly

All storage media (disks and tape) have to be treated with some care. Avoid placing them near heat or in very cold places, and keep them well away from liquids and dirt. Magnetic media, like floppy disks and standalone hard disks, can be damaged when placed next to strong magnetic forces or motors. Optical media, like CDs and DVDs, may seem more robust but can still deteriorate if kept in poor conditions.

When you pick up a CD or DVD hold it by the edges so that finger marks are not placed on the surface. Never touch the surface of magnetic media.

E-portfolio

For all but one of the units in this AS qualification you will be assessed by an e-portfolio. The exception is Unit 3, which is externally assessed. The e-portfolio will contain all your assessment work for a particular unit. You should design it to be viewed onscreen, using a standard web browser. There are five steps to consider when planning your portfolio and putting it together:

* *Step 1*: create an appropriate structure for the e-portfolio
* *Step 2*: collect together all the required information, converting files to an appropriate format if necessary
* *Step 3*: authenticate your work
* *Step 4*: provide a table of contents, using hyperlinks to locate information easily
* *Step 5*: test for size, compatibility and ease of use, ensuring that it conforms to the technical specification.

Step 1 Creating an appropriate structure

In the specification for each unit, check the assessment requirements. If you do not have a paper copy of the specification, you can download it from the Edexcel website. Read carefully the section headed 'Assessment Evidence'. You will also be able to see how your work will be judged in the section headed 'Assessment Criteria'. (Also, refer to the introductory section to each unit in this book.)

List all the evidence that you have to produce for the unit. These could be documents, websites, e-books, presentations, databases, videos, etc. You could make this into a checklist, and tick off each item as you produce it.

Decide on the order in which you would like to present the evidence, and create a folder structure for your e-portfolio accordingly.

Step 2 Collect together all the required information, converting files to an appropriate format

Check that you have covered all the assessment objectives for the unit.

You may have to convert your working files into appropriate formats. These would normally be:

* pdf format for documents that would normally be printed
* swf (Flash movie) format for animations
* jpg or png format for images
* html for onscreen presentations.

If your PowerPoint presentations include animations you should convert them to Flash format. If not, then convert them to html. You may include audio and video as well.

New suitable formats may become available during the course of your work, and you should check with your teacher whether they can be used.

Step 3 Authenticate your work

Teachers are expected to give you guidance as you are putting your e-portfolios together. They are required to note down any help they have given you that goes beyond the general help they have given to everyone in your teaching group. The level of their help is taken into account when assessing your work. Discuss with your teacher if you are at all unclear about the appropriate level of help that you should be receiving.

Your teacher should also monitor your work as it develops so that he or she can be sure that it is your own work. They will keep a checklist and/or witness statements to authenticate your work. You will need to include these in your e-portfolio. You could ask your teacher what he or she is doing to monitor and record this evidence.

Step 4 Provide a table of contents, using hyperlinks

You will present your e-portfolio with an introductory page in web format. The web page should be clear and businesslike. It should be viewable at 1024×768 pixels resolution. The introductory page should give:

* your name, candidate number and centre number

* an index of links to all the work contained in the e-portfolio. Each link can take the viewer to another web page or alternatively to any page or document in a suitable read-only format.

Step 5: Test for size, compatibility and ease of use

There are some important checks you need to carry out before submitting your e-portfolio for assessment. Check:

* how much memory the complete e-portfolio requires. You will be expected to use compression techniques to reduce the memory size of images and sounds

* that your e-portfolio displays correctly in a number of browsers, and on different types and sizes of screen

* that a viewer will find it easy to use and navigate – ask a fellow student to comment on this

* you have complied with the technical requirements for the relevant unit.

The information age

Introduction

Information communication technology (ICT) is advancing at such a rate it now impacts upon the majority of households and organisations in the developed world. This unit focuses on how ICT can enable users to access, exchange and use the information ICT is able to provide for social, economic and commercial purposes.

In particular, this unit investigates the Internet, the Internet's contribution to the 'information age' and the services it provides. Because ICT has had an enormous influence on personal, social and professional users in terms of working styles, employment opportunities, education, banking, shopping, entertainment, leisure, crime and legislation, the positive and negative aspects of ICT are also discussed in this unit. Finally, the unit will help you to develop your practical ICT skills as you conduct Internet-based research and use multimedia to develop an e-book.

What you need to learn

In completing this unit, you should achieve these learning outcomes:

* Know about the opportunities and issues of the 'information age'
* Understand the advantages and disadvantages of online services
* Have investigated e-books
* Be able to use a range of ICT tools and techniques such as e-books, website navigation and browser software
* Know how to create, develop and use an e-book.

Resource toolkit

To complete this unit, you need these essential resources:

* access to computer hardware including a printer, digital camera and scanner
* access to computer software, in particular Microsoft Word, Powerpoint and graphics and web authoring software
* access to the Internet and sufficient storage space.

How you will be assessed

This unit is internally assessed. Page vii explains what this means.

There are three assessment objectives:

AO1 Investigate aspects of the information age in which you live

AO2 Design and create an e-book to present your evidence and provide a snapshot of life in today's information age

AO3 Evaluate your e-book and your own performance.

To demonstrate your coverage of these assessment objectives, you will produce an e-portfolio of evidence, showing what you have learnt and what you can do:

(a) You will write a description and evaluation of at least five different types of online service, drawn together to give a picture of the current scope and limitations of the Internet as a whole.

(b) You will write a description of how ICT is affecting at least five different aspects of people's lives, considering the benefits and of life overall in the information age.

(c) You will include a description of at least three factors contributing to the digital divide and some of the measures being taken to bridge the gap, with an evaluation of the impact/extent of the digital divide, drawn together to give a picture of the current situation.

(d)/(e) Your e-book should include:

* your work for (a), (b), and (c)
* evidence that demonstrates your understanding of multimedia design principles and your ability to use software tools appropriately.
* some ready-made and some original multimedia components

(f) You should also include in your portfolio an evaluation of your e-book and your own performance on this unit.

How high can you aim?

The information age has provided a wealth of opportunities to almost all sectors of society. Through this unit, you will explore a range of issues associated with the benefits, issues and challenges of living in this information age. This unit will also identify some of the boundaries that the information age has generated to the extent of creating a digital divide between communities and countries. You will also be expected to embrace the information age and develop your own e-book and evaluate your own performance throughout this process.

This unit will be assessed internally and some of the **Assessment activities** provided can be used towards your e-portfolio. These contain **Assessment hints** on what you need to do to pass (✓), gain a better mark (✓✓) or get top marks (✓✓✓). For example, when identifying different online services available to home and business users, higher grades can be achieved by providing an in-depth evaluation of at least five different types of online service.

The assessment that covers ICT and how it affects your daily life, can feed into your e-portfolio evidence where at least five different aspects of people's lives need to be analysed in conjunction with how ICT has impacted upon them. Higher grades can be achieved by analysing the benefits and drawbacks of each to give a clear and balanced picture of life in the information age.

The research assessment into factors contributing to the digital divide will contribute to your evidence for your e-portfolio with the aim of describing at least three aspects of the digital divide (two global and one local). Higher grades can be achieved through analysis of the causes and effects of each and the measures taken to bridge the gap.

The creation of an e-book will allow you to use a range of multimedia tools and techniques and appropriate software tools. Higher grades can be achieved through originality in the selection and use of these tools in your e-book design.

Finally higher grades on the evaluation of the e-book assessment evidence can be achieved through the incorporation of user feedback, instead of just evaluative comments based on the key features.

Ready to start?

Why not keep a log of the time you take to complete this unit? Devise a blank form that you could use to record the time that you spend on this course.

1.1 The information age

Digital technologies are having a profound effect on the way individuals and businesses operate, and they are all part and parcel of this new, ever advancing information age. Information can be exchanged globally in milliseconds, shared between millions of users simultaneously and stored in devices no bigger than a pen.

Some of the benefits of, and opportunities created by, the information age are shown in Figure 1.1.

These opportunities exist because of a range of new technologies:

* the Internet
* multimedia
* broadband
* wireless
* digital and mobile technologies (for example, TV, video and telephones).

The Internet

The Internet is a network that links computers globally, thus enabling them to store and to transfer vast amounts of data. In order to access the Internet, a number of factors have to be considered, and these fall into three broad categories:

* hardware
* software
* services.

Initially, the hardware you needed to enable you to connect to the Internet included a computer and a modem, and access to a telephone line. However, the need for faster, more reliable connections has created more efficient ways of accessing the Internet (Figure 1.2).

Each method brings a host of benefits:

* you can use your landline to make telephone calls whilst you are surfing on the Internet
* faster connection speeds
* better reliability in terms of connecting and instant connection
* there is a permanent connection – you do not need continually to dial up.

Key term

The term *landline* is often used to describe a fixed telephone connection at home or work, a connection that travels over terrestrial circuits.

FIGURE 1.1 *The benefits and opportunities of the information age*

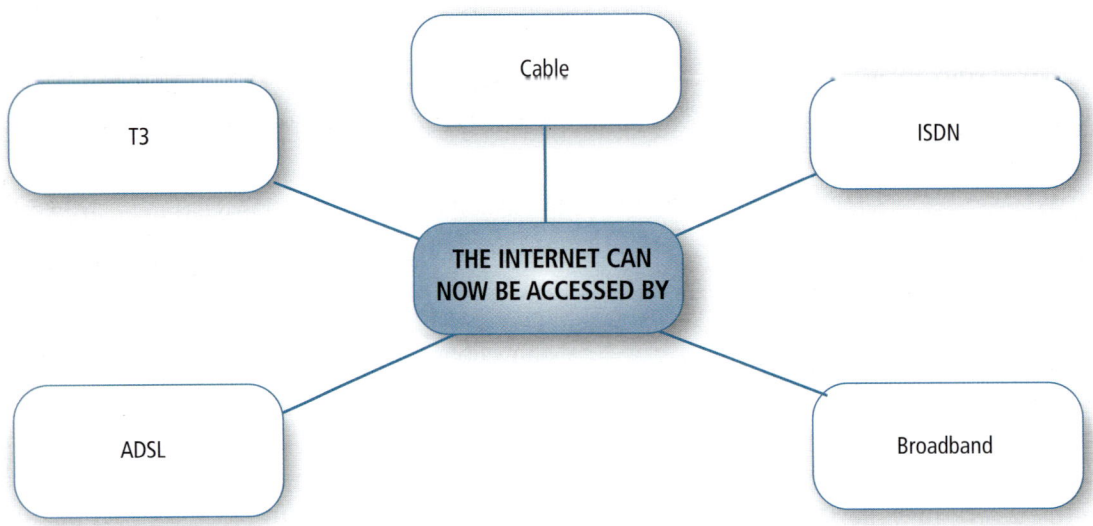

FIGURE 1.2 *Modern ways to access the Internet*

For some people, however, especially occasional users of the Internet, the additional costs associated with upgrading to a faster medium of connection do not make this a viable option and, for others, there is no alternative but to use a landline if these newer services are not provided in the area where they live. In recent years, however, newer and more accessible systems have become widely available, which means that users now do not even need a computer to connect with the Internet. In this advanced information age, users who cannot access the Internet via a traditional PC can use alternative technologies (Figure 1.3).

In terms of software, most operating systems today have integrated Internet access software that includes dial-up networking and browsers. Once access to the Internet has been gained via an ISP (internet service provider), a number of services are available to users:

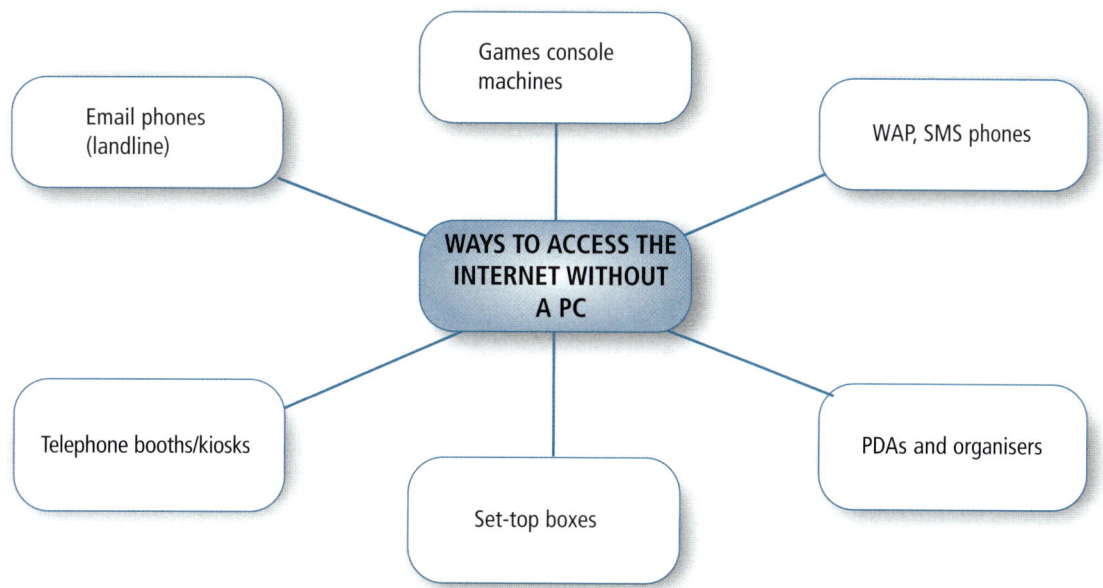

FIGURE 1.3 *Alternative ways to access the Internet*

* e-mail
* web browsing
* file transfer protocol (FTP)
* newsgroups
* internet relay chat (IRC).

> **Key term**
>
> *File transfer protocol (FTP)* is the protocol (set of rules) used for exchanging files over the Internet.

In addition, other services may be available from an ISP, including web space, web hosting and helpdesk support.

Multimedia

Multimedia tools can be used to generate sounds, moving images, pictures and graphics. Multimedia can enhance documents, presentations, web pages and e-books, etc. The ability to download sounds, pictures and clips and use scanning and photographic facilities has played a major role in the creation of e-books and other dynamic documents.

Broadband

Broadband is a very high-speed connection to the Internet that is always active (i.e. on). It has a much larger capacity than a traditional landline to receive and send data (up to 10 or 20 times faster than a 56 K modem, thus allowing you to view web content and download files more quickly). A number of providers offer broadband services – PIPEX (Figure 1.4) being just one of these.

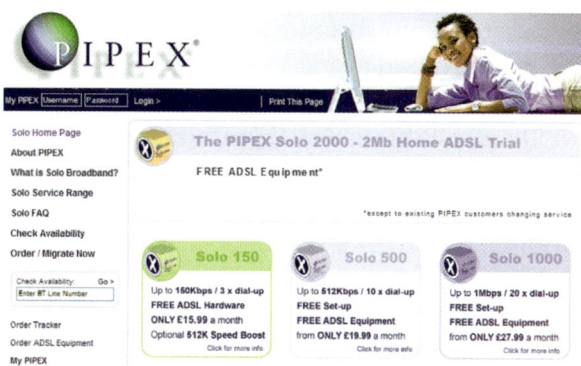

FIGURE 1.4 *PIPEX home page*

Wireless, digital and mobile technologies

> **Key term**
>
> *Wireless technology* operates without the use of cables (i.e. wires) needing to be attached to a hardware device, thus making the use of the device more flexible.

UNIT 1: THE INFORMATION AGE

There is a wide range of wireless technologies available. Some of these are designed to meet the needs of businesses, such as:

* local wireless
* wireless networks (WLAN)
* mobile phone networks.

Local wireless incorporates cordless products, such as keyboards and mice that use infrared or radio technologies. This provides a certain element of flexibility, providing connectivity within range of the desktop. One of the more versatile types of radio technology is 'Bluetooth'. Bluetooth technology facilitates communication between mobile phones, PDAs, PCs and other PC-related devices within a range of 10 metres.

Mobile phone networks are used for much more than voice calls. The capability and sophistication of handsets and networks' increased data transfer speeds has enabled the development of more dynamic, innovative devices.

Wireless networks operate without the need for cables; they offer the same benefits as traditional cabled networks, but without the restrictions and confinements for users. Devices that are WLAN-enabled, such as laptops, can be connected at anytime, providing they are within range. Wireless networks are more advanced than local wireless in terms of the range available.

The growth of wireless, digital and mobile technologies is evident in the range of ICT devices now available. Wireless and mobile technologies (such as laptops, PDAs and wireless networks) mean you are not restricted to working in a conventional environment, such as an office. These technologies enable people to work from home, on the move or in another branch of the same organisation.

Digital television and video

Digital television (DTV) is the transmission of television signals using digital rather than conventional analog methods. The advantages of DTV over analog TV include:

* superior image resolution (detail) for a given bandwidth
* smaller bandwidth for a given image resolution
* compatibility with computers and the Internet
* interactivity
* superior audio quality
* consistency of reception over varying distances.

Digital video is part of digital versatile disc (DVD), a new optical disc technology. The DVD holds 4.7 gigabytes of information on one of its two sides, or enough for a 133-minute movie. With two layers on each of its two sides, it will hold up to 17 gigabytes of video, audio or other information.

The opportunities of the information age

The information age has provided many opportunities, some of which are described below.

The presentation of information

Businesses and other organisations can create templates that can be used on a national or even global basis, and multimedia tools offer the ability to produce designs that are more creative and visual (for example, on websites or in presentations at conferences or meetings).

> **Key term**
>
> A *template* is a master document that can be used again and again. For example, a company may create templates of letters, reports and other documents all employees must use in their communications with clients or customers. Each template will contain basic information that can be changed for the particular circumstances. Templates are designed carefully so that the company presents the same image to all its customers and, in this way, it can control how it appears to the outside world.

Sharing information quickly

Rapid information sharing has been enabled through such technologies as webcams, email, video conferencing and the emergence of virtual communities set up on the Internet that offer newsgroups and chat rooms, etc. The facilities of mobile phone technology to send and receive pictures or text have also contributed to the speed at which data and information are communicated.

Greater interaction with others and organisations

This has again been achieved through technologies that have enabled effective and speedy interactions. The emphasis on 'collaborative' working environments and work spaces, where people share ideas and data, has had an impact of the types of software that are being marketed to organisations – for example, e-mail, intranets, extranets and the Internet now make more dynamic interaction across organisations, and even across communities, possible. Such devices as laptops, PDAs and mobile phones permit people to be more flexible in the places where they choose to work: indeed, more and more workers are now home rather than office based. ICT has thus helped to overcome the barriers of geographical distance: colleagues can communicate with each other instantly from almost all parts of the world.

Business opportunities large and small

The information age has created a more flexible and open marketplace for businesses. Many small companies that could not possibly afford to set up and trade conventionally have been given the opportunity to trade online. For example, specialist suppliers of such goods as cheese, chocolate and wines can advertise their range of goods on their websites, and customers may browse and order online. These suppliers no longer need to be located near their customers and can operate with the minimum number of staff.

Virtual communities

These have been created as a result of the Internet bringing people together – people who share the same interests, hobbies, views and opinions. Virtual communities are held together by a sense of purpose and belonging (for example, communities that have been set up on the Internet to provide help and support for school children or to give them homework advice).

Mobile technologies

These range from PDAs to laptops and mobile phones. The capabilities of mobile technologies have enabled people to work and socialise on the move.

A self-service environment is what online consumers expect

With the growth in online shopping, banking and learning, in many cases it has become the 'norm' to click a button to carry out a transaction or to download information. Now you can store your personal details on websites, consumers do not even have to key in delivery or payment details, thus enabling them to be completely self-sufficient in their purchases.

> **Think it over...**
>
> We now expect things to be available wherever and whenever we want them. Think about what life would be like without computers, without Internet access, without mobile phones, without digital television and access to Sky, etc.

Issues and challenges arising from the information age

The information age has made people more aware of the implications of living and working within a society driven by communication technologies. The challenges people who live in this community face include:

* the need to be lifelong learners
* privacy rights
* copyright and legislation
* impacts on employment
* the digital divide.

Lifelong learners

'Lifelong learners' is a concept that has become a reality in this new information age. Learners from all generations can now gain access to learning resources, training opportunities, online courses and educational materials. The ability to download materials and to use the support of online tutors has given many people who were possibly prevented from studying via conventional methods new opportunities. The expectations of employers with regards to the skills base of their employees has also increased, resulting in a demand for more flexible 'knowledge workers'. This demand has driven many people into a continuous cycle of studying so that they become more 'marketable'.

Privacy rights

As more and more information is passed quickly between users and, in some cases, stored permanently on PCs, we all need to be aware of the legal issues surrounding the protection of data, privacy and the security of information, copyright and other legislative measures.

The Data Protection Act 1998

The Data Protection Act applies to the processing of personal information by any means, electronic or paper-based. The Act places obligations on people (data controllers) who collect, process and store personal records about consumers or customers

> **Key terms**
>
> *Data controllers* are those who control the contents of and use of, a collection of personal data. They can be any type of company or organisation, large or small, within the public or private sector. A data controller need not necessarily own a computer.
>
> *Data subjects* are the individuals to whom the personal data relates.

CASE STUDY

ChoicePoint stops selling some personal data
By Paul Roberts

Embattled personal data vendor ChoicePoint Inc. said on Friday that it will stop selling sensitive consumer data to many of its customers, except when that data helps complete a consumer transaction or helps government or law enforcement, the company said in a statement.

The company decided to stop selling sensitive data, such as Social Security numbers and driver's license numbers after being tricked into divulging personal information on about 145,000 people to identity thieves who posed as customers, according to a statement attributed to ChoicePoint Chairman and Chief Executive Officer (CEO) Derek V. Smith.

"These changes are a direct result of the recent fraud activity, our review . . . of our experience and products, and the response of consumers who have made it clear to us that they do not approve of sensitive personal data being used without direct benefit to them," Smith said in the statement, which was posted on ChoicePoint's Web site.

From now on, ChoicePoint will only sell sensitive personal information to customers when the data is necessary to complete a transaction, to accredited corporate customers that will use the data for user authentication or fraud prevention, or to help federal, state and local government and criminal justice agencies, ChoicePoint said.

The move, which should be complete within 90 days, will eliminate a number of "information products" that the company now sells to its customers, especially small businesses, the company said.

ChoicePoint also said it is creating an independent office of credentialing compliance and privacy. The office will oversee ChoicePoint's overhaul of the company's customer credentialing process, which was blamed for allowing identity thieves to register as legitimate customers and order personal information, the company said in its statement.

The Industry Standard

(data subjects). It also gives individuals certain rights regarding the information held about them.

Principles of good practice for data controllers

The Act sets out eight principles of good practice for data controllers. These are that data must be:

* fairly and lawfully processed
* processed for limited purposes
* adequate, relevant and not excessive
* accurate and up to date
* not kept longer than necessary
* processed in accordance with the individual's rights
* secure
* not transferred to countries outside the European Economic area unless the country has adequate protection for the individual.

Rights for individuals

The Act gives rights to individuals in respect of personal data held about them by data controllers. These include the rights to:

* *Subject access*: this allows people to find out what information is held about them on computer and within some manual records.
* *Prevent processing*: anyone can ask a data controller not to process information relating to him or her that causes substantial unwarranted damage or distress to them or anyone else.
* *Prevent processing for direct marketing*: anyone can ask a data controller not to process information relating to him or her for direct marketing purposes.
* *Automated decision-taking*: individuals have a right to object to decisions made only by automatic means, i.e. where there is no human involvement.
* *Compensation*: an individual can claim compensation from a data controller for damage and distress caused by any breach of the Act. Compensation for distress alone can only be claimed in limited circumstances.
* *Rectification, blocking, erasure and destruction*: individuals can apply to the court to order a data controller to rectify, block or destroy personal details if they are inaccurate or contain expressions of opinion based on inaccurate information.
* *Ask the Commissioner to assess whether the Act has been contravened*: if someone believes their personal information has not been processed in accordance with the Act, they can ask the Commissioner to make an assessment. If the Act is found to have been breached and the matter cannot be settled informally, an enforcement notice may be served on the data controller in question.

The Act does provide wide exemptions for journalistic, artistic, or literary purposes that would otherwise be in breach of the law.

Key terms

Personal data refers to information about living, identifiable individuals. Personal data does not have to be particularly sensitive information and can be as little as name and address.

Automatically processed means processed by computer or other technology such as documents image-processing systems.

The role of the Information Commissioner

The Information Commissioner is an independent supervisory authority which has both national and international roles. Primarily the Commissioner is responsible for ensuring that the Data Protection Act and the Freedom of Information Act are enforced.

In the UK, the Commissioner's duties include:

* promoting good information handling
* encouraging codes of practice for data controllers
* serving information notices which require data controllers to provide information in order to assess their compliance with the Act
* enforcing the Act where a breach of the law occurs

In order to carry out these duties, the Commissioner maintains a public register of data controllers, which includes information about the controller such as their name, address and a description of the processing of the personal data to be carried out.

Register of data controllers

Anyone processing personal information, with a few exceptions, must notify the Commissioner's Office that they are doing so, giving their name, address and broad descriptions of:

* those about whom personal data are held
* the items of data held
* the purposes for which the data are used
* the sources from which the information may be disclosed i.e. shown or passed to
* any overseas countries or territories to which the data may be transferred.

For more information about the Data Protection Act, see Unit 2 and the Information Commissioner's website (a link to the site is available at www.heinemann.co.uk/hotlinks (express code 2008P).

Computer Misuse Act 1990

The Computer Misuse Act was enforced to address the increased threat of hackers trying to gain unauthorised access to computer systems. Prior to this Act there was minimal protection, and there were difficulties in prosecuting hackers because theft of data in this way was not considered to be a deprivation to the owner. There a number of offences and penalties under this Act.

Offences

* *Unauthorised access*: an attempt by a hacker to gain unauthorised access to a computer system
* *Unauthorised access with the intention of committing another offence*: on gaining access a hacker will then continue with the intent of committing a further crime
* *Unauthorised modification of data or programs*: introducing viruses to a computer system is a criminal offence. Guilt is assessed by the level of intent to cause disruption, or to impair the processes of a computer system.

Penalties

* *Unauthorised access*: imprisonment for up to six months and/or a fine of up to £2,000
* *Unauthorised access with the intention of committing another offence*: imprisonment for up to five years and/or an unlimited fine
* *Unauthorised modification*: imprisonment for up to five years and/or an unlimited fine.

Copyright and legislation

Copyright is awarded automatically to a product (be it a book, a painting or a piece of software) immediately it is completed; no further action is required in order to activate copyright. Copyright is transferable if the originator/author grants it and it can exist for up to fifty years following the death of the originator/author.

The are a number of copyright issues concerning software. First is software piracy – the copying of software to be used on more machines than the individual licences allow for. Secondly is ownership – if a piece of software has been developed for a specific organisation, the copyright remains with the developer unless conditions to the contrary have been written into a contract. Finally is transference – can an employee who has developed a piece of software for his or her organisation take the ownership and copyright with him or her to another organisation? Again, unless this is addressed in the employee's contract, the organisation will have no right to any software the employee has developed.

Copyright, Designs and Patent Act

The Copyright, Designs and Patent Act provides protection to software developers and organisations against unauthorised copying of their software, designs, printed material and any other products. Under copyright legislation, an organisation or developer can ensure that its intellectual property (IP) has been safeguarded against those who wish to exploit and make gains from the originator's research and developments.

> **Key terms**
>
> A person's or organisation's *intellectual property (IP)* is their ideas, inventions or 'creativity' (for example, the work of writers or artists). It is protected, for example, by patents, trade marks and copyright, which give the owner *intellectual property rights (IPR)* to protect their 'property' under the Copyright, Designs and Patents Act.

Software piracy can be broken down into a number of key areas:

- *Recordable CD-ROMs*: Pirates copy large amounts of software on to one recordable CD-ROM and make multiple copies of this CD-ROM.
- *Professional counterfeits*: These are professionally made copies of software, including media packages, licences and even security holograms. They are made to resemble the genuine article.
- *Internet piracy*: The downloading or distribution of software on the Internet that infringes any copyright laws.
- *Corporate overuse*: This occurs when organisations install software package(s) on to more machines than they have licences for.
- *Hard disk loaders*: Unscrupulous retail outlets or dealers load illegal versions of software on to computer systems to encourage customers to buy their computer hardware. Customers will not have the appropriate licences or be entitled to other services, such as technical support or upgrades.

The Federation Against Software Theft (FAST) was set up in 1984 by the software industry with the aim of preventing software piracy. Anybody caught breaching the copyright law would be prosecuted under this federation.

Impact on employment

The information age has had a profound impact upon employment. The move towards automated jobs has led to a rise in the demand for 'knowledge workers' – employees who have the required level of skills to operate a computer, to input data, extract information, manipulate data sheets, and to design and develop applications, documents, programs and websites. For some workers, the information age has meant that a lack of these skills has hindered their promotion and has even forced some employees out of their jobs. For employers, the challenges that face them are costly, both financially and in terms of time and resources.

Investment in newer technologies has impacted upon the working environment, leading to more workplace legislation and health and safety requirements. In addition, more resources have had to be channelled into the training and development of staff so that full advantage can be taken of these technologies.

The digital divide

The 'digital divide' is the term used to describe how people can be excluded from the online world. People may not be able to go online because they do not have the money, the knowledge or the hardware or software. People may also be excluded because they fear the new technology, because they feel they are too old to learn new skills or because they have a physical or mental disability. For whatever reason people are prevented from going online, there is a divide between those who can and those who cannot. Those who can benefit from all those things ICT can offer (access to the Internet, online shopping and banking, etc.); those who cannot are prevented from enjoying these benefits.

This divide is very apparent all over the world, but in some countries it is compensated for to a certain extent by people having access to some forms of technology. An example of this can be seen in the rise in mobile phone ownership. In some households, even those in the most deprived areas of the world, mobile phone ownership is considered to be the 'norm'. In other parts of the world, most households also have access to digital or satellite television.

Think it over...

In some parts of the world, having fresh water each day would be considered to be a luxury, especially if you didn't have to walk miles and miles to get it. In other parts of the world, fresh water is taken for granted, and having a computer, Internet access and a mobile phone is also taken for granted. Having the luxury and choice to watch, shop, entertain, learn and develop using ICT is still unfortunately dictated by where you live and how much money you have.

Knowledge check

1. How has the Internet revolutionised the way in which we communicate?
2. What is meant by the term 'multimedia'?
3. What opportunities have been created by the 'information age'?
4. What are the benefits of using broadband?

1.2 Online services

A vast range of online services is available on the Internet (Figure 1.5), and these services have become very accessible. Because the Internet provides a global gateway that can be accessed by home and business users, the Internet presents many opportunities:

* more advanced, quicker and cheaper communication links for individuals, businesses and the government
* access to real-time information
* the ability to shop, bank, educate and entertain
* the ability to download and archive a range of multimedia products and services.

Communication

In the digital age, communication (and whom you communicate with) has no geographical boundaries.

> **Key term**
>
> A *global gateway* is a gateway that can be accessed, at any time, anywhere (providing you have the necessary hardware and software) and by anyone. It is an international network of information and resources that is not restricted by geographical or cultural boundaries.

The services provided by the Internet have enabled people to use a range of communication media:

* e-mail
* instant messaging and chat services
* newsgroups
* online conferencing
* blogs.

E-mail

E-mail has become one of the fastest and most widely accessible forms of communication in recent years. E-mail is no longer a matter of sitting

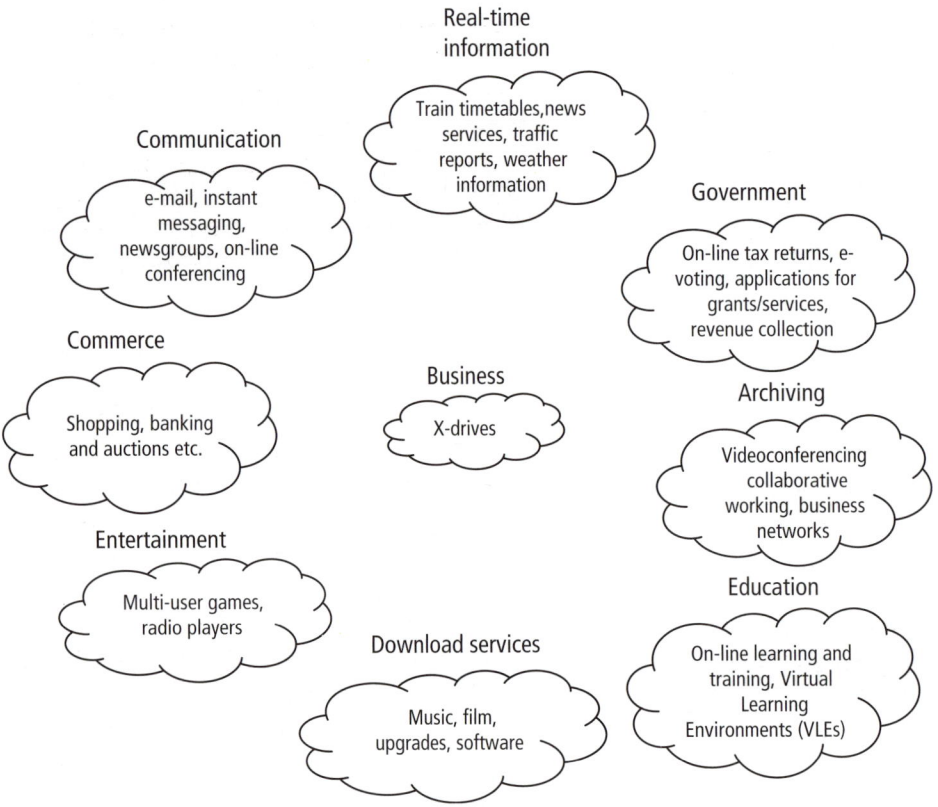

FIGURE 1.5 *The services available on the Internet*

down in front of a computer terminal and tapping commands into a keyboard. New and more portable tools are now available: games consoles, WAP phones, digital televisions and set-top boxes.

The advantages of using e-mail include:

* *Speed*: you can send messages immediately to anywhere in the world at the touch of the button.
* *Multiple sends and copies*: you can send the same message to many recipients.
* *Cost*: the costs are minimal and, in some instances, to e-mail may be free (for example, if you send e-mails from some educational establishments).
* *Convenience*: you can communicate 24 hours a day, 7 days a week.
* *Sharing data*: because the same information can be transferred to many users, these users have access to the same attached files, graphics and moving images, etc.
* *Ease of use*: once you are familiar with some of the basic functions of an e-mail package, it is very easy to send and receive e-mails because the system is icon driven.

There are a number of other benefits to e-mail. You can keep a historical record (audit) of the messages you have sent and received. Your messages can also be saved into different formats, updated and printed out if required. E-mail contains a range of multimedia elements that allow you to send messages containing graphics, sound, moving images and even hyperlinks to Internet pages.

The disadvantages of e-mail mainly concern technical and security issues, such as the following:

* *Spamming*: spam e-mails are unwanted messages you are sent by advertisers and unknown users who broadcast their messages universally to an entire address book.
* *Routing*: e-mail is not always sent direct from A to B; it can be routed to other destinations before it finally reaches the receiver(s). Routing can cause a number of problems. For example, it takes more time before the message reaches its destination, and there are more opportunities for the message to be intercepted. The message may also become distorted or lost.
* *Security*: an e-mail can be easily intercepted unless you have applied some form of encryption to the message.

Key term

Encryption software scrambles message transmissions. When a message is encrypted, a secret numerical code is applied – an 'encryption key' – and the message is transmitted or stored in indecipherable characters. The message can only be read after it has been reconstructed through the use of a 'matching key'. Some Internet-based companies use encryption software to protect sensitive user information and also to authenticate passwords that have been sent to a user to set-up new accounts, etc.

CASE STUDY

Bill Gates gets 4 million emails a day
David Teather in New York
Friday November 19, 2004
The Guardian

The next time you're sifting through the mortgage offers, cheap Rolex watches or dubious business proposals from Nigeria, spare a thought for Bill Gates. The Microsoft founder is the most spammed man in the world, with 4m emails arriving in his inbox each day.

Steve Ballmer, Microsoft's chief executive, told a conference in Singapore that being the world's best-known software billionaire has its down side: "Bill receives 4m pieces of email per day, most of it spam."

The upside of the Microsoft founder's bulging inbox is that it appears to have focused his mind on the problem.

Spam is regarded as perhaps the biggest threat to the internet, with some experts putting it as high as 80% of the world's online traffic.

* *Confidentiality*: because an e-mail can be lost, intercepted or distorted, it is not deemed appropriate to send confidential messages via e-mail.

Instant messaging and chat services

There is a wide range of messaging and chat services available to all types of business and home users. Some of these services are tailored to meet individual needs and requirements. For example, business community chat services are marketed at specific types of business organisations and educational messaging services provide updates on training and educational developments. These services are similar to forums in that they provide an environment where people can share and swap ideas.

For home users, the range of services is extensive. For example, facilities such as MSN and Yahoo Messenger© (Figures 1.6 and 1.7) allow subscribers to join specialist user groups. Users are then able to monitor who is available online and can chat with individuals from their list.

Newsgroups

Newsgroups can be described as 'interactive discussion forums'. They allow users who share the same interests or research areas to communicate across the Internet, an intranet or an extranet system (Figure 1.8). Newsgroups are very interactive in that people respond, post facts and ideas, and view current articles that have been included on the site (Figure 1.9). Examples of different categories of newsgroups include:

* online games/gaming sites
* environmental protection
* fan-sites for pop singers or football clubs.

FIGURE 1.6 *MSN Messenger*

FIGURE 1.7 *Yahoo! Messenger*

FIGURE 1.8 *Excite newsgroups*

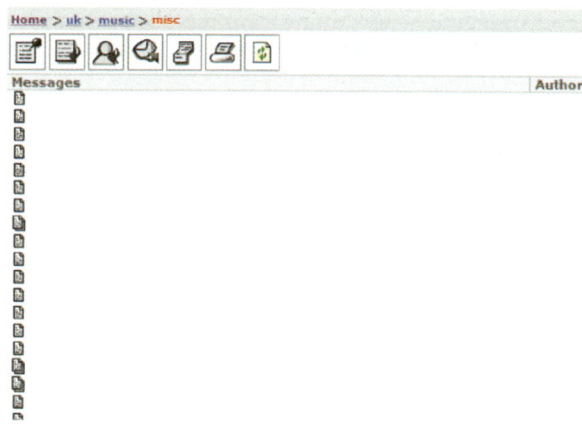

FIGURE 1.9 *Messages posted on a site*

Think it over...

There are a number of ways that people can communicate online, using chat rooms and messaging services, subscribing to newsgroups and forums.

Over a period of one week, track how many times you are invited to chat online with a friend, and note how long you actually spend chatting online. In addition, have a look at a forum that is of interest to you, for example, online games, a hobby, music or film topic. Over the course of a week, see how many postings are made and the types of questions that are presented to forum members.

At the end of the week report your findings to the rest of your class.

Online conferencing

Key term

Online conferencing allows people to share information with large audiences, interactively and cost effectively, thus eliminating the need to travel to meetings. For example it can bring employees together for training sessions, or it can bring suppliers and customers closer to the organisations they deal with.

Blogs

A blog is a web page that serves as a publicly accessible personal journal for an individual.

Key term

Blog is shortened form of 'weblog'.

Real-time information

The ability to view regularly updated news and train, bus and flight timetables, weather reports and sporting results online has improved the quality of information for people who are travelling or who require constantly updated information. People and organisations who want to be able to plan a journey online by viewing travel times have created a huge demand for sites that offer these facilities, such as ferryport.com (Figure 1.10).

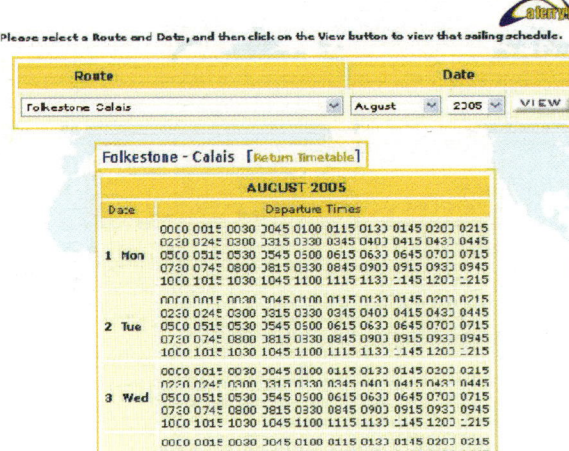

FIGURE 1.10 *P&O Ferries Folkestone to Calais timetable*

It is also now possible to listen to radio programmes in real-time, as well as still being able to listen to recently recently aired programmes.

Commerce

E-commerce has had a profound effect on the way that we shop and bank. It has provided flexibility and in many cases cost-effectiveness to high-street shopping.

In shopping, e-commerce has created more choice. We can view a range of products in online stores, compare prices and make informed choices about our purchases. In addition payments can be made easily and securely online.

Auction sites, such as ebay.co.uk, have grown rapidly over the last few years. Almost anything and everything seems to be on sale, from film props, to food items, rare memorabilia to modern books, CDs, DVDs and other merchandise.

Banking has also adopted online service provision. Almost every bank has a website where information can be viewed and downloaded, personal accounts activated, loans arranged and transactions carried out.

Government

You can now carry out many interactions with government departments online. For example, you can:

* book your driving test (see Figure 1.11)
* apply for a passport
* claim Child Benefit
* fill in your Income Tax return and pay any tax you owe
* get health advice
* find out about your rights as an employee and many, many more things.

For some tasks, such as applying for an Educational Maintenance Grant, you do have to fill in a paper form and post it with supporting documents. In all these cases you can download the forms and read the information about them online.

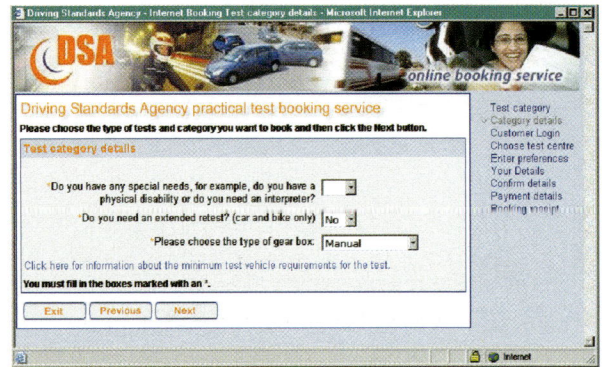

FIGURE 1.11 *Booking a driving test on the Driving Standards Agency website (a link to the site is available at www.heinemann.co.uk/hotlinks, express code 2008P)*

Each government service has its own website, but you can find your way to the right one from the Directgov site (www.directgov.gov.uk).

From Directgov you will also be able to locate your local council's website, where you should be able to:

* report graffiti
* book adult education classes
* raise a petition
* respond to a consultation
* express your views about local issues
* pay council tax

At election time you may be able to vote online, or to register your vote at a voting machine; this is known as e-voting.

You should be able to find out easily online who your elected representatives (Members of Parliament and councillors) are. Many have their own websites, and all can be contacted by email.

> **Theory into practice**
>
> Check what services are offered online on your local council website.
>
> Find out who your local councillors are and how to contact them.

Education

There is a wide range of online services that have been set up to support education, training and development. The creation of VLEs (Virtual Learning Environments) and the growth in online organisations that promote courses and qualifications such as Learn Direct, CISCO and ECDL (European Computer Driving Licence) qualifications, have enabled wider participation for learners who cannot physically get to a place of learning. The ability to work through course materials and study online has also helped to support different types of learners who may have difficulties with keeping up in a class environment, or for those learners who do not feel challenged enough and can work through at a more advanced pace.

> **Key term**
>
> A *Virtual Learning Environment (VLE)* is an environment that has been set-up to promote online learning based on flexibility and choice. Learners can download material, view course material and lectures, and submit assessments to specific learning areas that have been securely set up.

Business

Online services have improved the efficiency, cost-effectiveness, competitiveness and productivity of some businesses. Videoconferencing has enabled businesses from across the world to sit in on meetings and training events and to be able to take part in decision-making processes within a matter of seconds. Online services have also promoted a culture of collaborative working within departments and throughout all the branches of organisations that operate on a worldwide scale.

Business networks have been set up at various levels to support multinational corporations through to single business users. These networks offer support and advice on a range of business and financial issues to encourage the use and sharing of good practice as a business standard. For some business users, these networks provide a lifeline to what's actually happening in business communities, especially if they are constrained geographically and feel quite cut off from the city or other local businesses.

Entertainment

> **Theory into practice**
>
> Use *Search* to find out what is happening in your area this weekend. Widen your search to further afield if necessary to discover what is on at cinemas, theatres, concert halls, sports grounds, etc. You may find the websites of your local newspapers, radio and TV stations useful for this.

The ability to access radio, news, video clips and games (Figure 1.12) online has created more opportunities for people to interact socially with other people and to keep people up to date with developments in entertainment.

In addition, single or multi-user online gaming (from such things as role playing to chess) has united certain groups of people into cultures that are not geographically divided and that are driven by interactivity and social participation.

FIGURE 1.12 An interactive online game at Weboggle (a link to the site is available at www.heinemann.co.uk/hotlinks, express code 2008P)

Key terms

Single user games are played individually. *Multi user games* are designed to be played by a number of users, usually in real-time.

Download services and archiving

The ability to download information (such as upgrades, software and entertainment files) has enabled people to access resources at the touch of a button. Once this information has been downloaded, it can be archived for future use. Information can now also be accessed and shared on an x-drive, that enables information to be stored in a designated area on the Web allowing access at anytime.

You can archive information (for example, a link, a web address or web page, etc.) temporarily or permanently on removable storage media (DVDs, CD-ROMs, etc.) or in Favorites or on your hard disk drive. Archiving information allows you to keep track and register pages that you have viewed for future reference. This information can then be accessed easily, downloaded and used as and when required.

Theory into practice

Explore and evaluate a range of different services available online. Find three examples of both Internet and non-Internet based services for:

* a training or education service
* a travel agent or holiday booking company.

For both the Internet and non-Internet based services, evaluate:

1. Their target audiences (i.e. the people whom they expect will use this service)
2. The benefits and drawbacks of using the service in this way (i.e. Internet versus non-Internet)
3. Whether the service is fit for its purpose (i.e. does it achieve what it set out to achieve?)
4. Any possible amendments you could make to the service to improve its effectiveness.

Which of the two (i.e. Internet or non-Internet) do you think offers the best service? Give the reasons for your conclusion.

Assessment activity

There are a number of online services available to both home and business users. For the following sets of users, identify three different online services they could use. When you have identified the services, complete a copy of Table 1.1. You can substitute some of the criteria for your own if necessary.

Users:

* a student
* a business that has branches across Europe
* a retired person.

Assessment hint

✓ Provide a description with some evaluative comments of the online services available.

✓✓ Provide a description with some in-depth evaluation of the online services.

STUDENT	BUSINESS	RETIRED
Type of service 1 2 3	Type of service 1 2 3	Type of service 1 2 3
Benefits of service 1 2 3	Benefits of service 1 2 3	Benefits of service 1 2 3
Ease of use 1 2 3	Ease of use 1 2 3	Ease of use 1 2 3
Example of service (site) 1 2 3	Example of service (site) 1 2 3	Example of service (site) 1 2 3

TABLE 1.1 *Online services and different types of user*

Signpost for e-portfolio evidence

Save this work in your e-portfolio. It could contribute towards covering evidence (a).

Knowledge check

1 List three online services.
2 What are the advantages and disadvantages of using e-mail?

1.3 Life in the information age

ICT has had an enormous impact on the way people do things in their personal, professional and social lives. The effects of the information age can now be felt in such areas of life as:

* working styles
* communication
* education
* entertainment and leisure
* banking and shopping
* decision-making
* employment opportunities
* crime and crime prevention
* civil rights
* legislation.

Working styles

ICT has had a tremendous effect on work styles and the way in which everyday tasks are carried out in organisations. ICT has also affected the way in which data is processed, information is transmitted and knowledge is applied. Similarly, ICT has influenced the physical environment of the workplace (for example, most offices are now designed to accommodate individual workstations), what workers do, where they are based, their job roles, their interaction with other people and their needs for skills updating (for example, they must be trained to operate computers and in the features of the software they use).

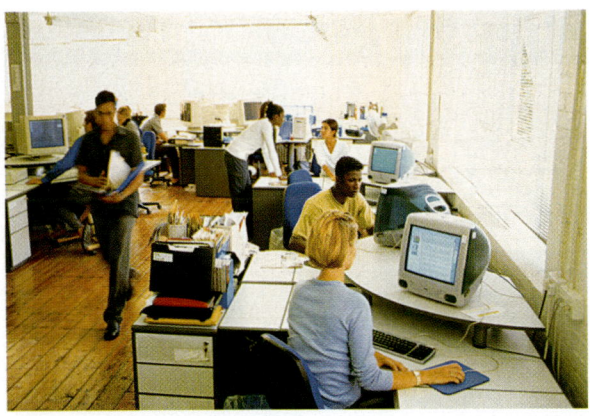

Most offices are now designed to accommodate individual workstations

Communication

ICT has affected not only the way people communicate and but also the means of communication. In today's society, the preferred method of communication is either e-mail or chat, messenger and text facilities. The emphasis now is on speed, interactivity and collaboration. For example, Word permits people to add comments to a document without changing the wording of the document. This document can then be sent as an attachment to other people who can similarly add their comments. When the changes to the document have been agreed by all concerned, the comments can either be incorporated into the document or disregarded.

Education

The effects of ICT on education have been felt at all levels of learning. For example, the National Curriculum requires that children can use computers from an early age and are proficient in applications software as they progress into secondary, further and higher education. Pupils are encouraged to use ICT in nearly all the subject areas they study, from English and maths to art and foreign languages.

To support the teaching of ICT in schools and colleges, a number of initiatives have been set up to provide them with the resources they need to deliver this teaching. For example, reduced-price computers for teachers and laptops for teaching purposes have been introduced in an attempt to promote wider access to ICT and, hopefully, to encourage new ways of delivering the knowledge the pupils need. Support from local county councils to get schools connected to the Internet and to provide them with hardware and software for classrooms has also contributed to widening participation in ICT.

The impact of ICT on education has been a positive one as children and students are taught practical ICT skills that are transferable to the workplace. ICT has also filtered into other academic and training organisations, providing opportunities for all levels and ages of learner. For example, e-learning has risen in popularity as more and more people have become aware of such online courses as ECDL (European Computer Driving Licence), Learn Direct and Webwise.

Entertainment and leisure

Entertainment and leisure pursuits have changed in terms of what we do and how we do it. These changes are primarily due to the Internet, which provides endless opportunities for people to communicate, play games and be involved in interactive pursuits. The Internet also allows people to plan their leisure activities online by enabling them to book tickets for flights, concerts, attractions and holidays. In addition, such technologies as mobile phones and games consoles have contributed to the changes in the way people are now entertained.

Banking and shopping

ICT has changed the way people bank and shop. Some of these changes can be considered to be part of an older technology (such as ATM machines (the 'holes in the wall') and electronic data capture at the point of sale in shops). However, recent changes and advances in ICT have opened up new opportunities for both commercial and retail organisations and their customers. These opportunities include:

- online banking
- online ordering
- online payments
- over-the-phone transactions and services, such as:
  - mortgages
  - setting up accounts
  - payments
  - orders
- automatic stock control and processing systems
- the introduction of loyalty schemes based on information gathered from bar-code products and customer data (for example, Tesco's and other supermarkets' loyalty cards).

Decision-making

To a certain extent, the decision-making process has become more automated in the information age. Certain decisions, especially within organisations, have been taken away from individuals and have become part of an electronic process based on data, statistics, forecasting and analysis. For example, loan companies will assess how much money someone may borrow based on data fed into a software program, and the designs for some new products are tested via computer simulations, which will highlight any modifications that need to be made to the product.

At a personal level, the decision-making process has also been changed. For example, a decision to book a holiday before the information age might have involved physically visiting a travel agent, searching through brochures, paying a deposit, going back to make the final payment, being sent your tickets, etc. – a process that could have taken months. In the information age, however, this process can be reduced to a matter of minutes, and it can save you hundreds if not thousands of pounds – all with the click of a button.

Employment opportunities

In terms of employment opportunities, the impact of ICT on the banking sector, for example, has been both positive and negative, as Table 1.2 shows.

The demands of e-commerce now require organisations to provide electronic and online facilities for payment methods, ordering and transaction services. Those organisations that fail to supply these facilities often suffer in terms of a shift in customer loyalty to more dynamic organisations that do provide these facilities.

At the end of the day, pension, financial and other specialist advisers are being replaced by intelligent systems and competent operators who can navigate their way through menu systems and decision tables.

POSITIVE	NEGATIVE
More streamlined and efficient service (people are available at the end of a phone or computer)	Loss of personal one-to-one service, no need to speak to somebody in person (e.g. bank manager)
Greater flexibility (e.g. wider payment options, able to shop around for the best deals and compare prices, etc.)	Could lead to a loss in jobs or unwanted changes in job roles
More choice in products and services available (online)	Not everybody feels comfortable with using ICT facilities to bank and would prefer a personal service
Convenience (you do not have to leave home for mortgage advice or to transfer funds, etc.)	Smaller branches may be forced to close, especially ones located in rural areas

TABLE 1.2 *The impact of ICT on banking*

Crime and crime prevention, civil rights and legislation

As has already been noted in this unit, ICT has impacted on almost every area of our lives. However, the rapid rate at which ICT is being embraced by almost everyone has caused some concerns about how we can ensure we are working within a secure environment. You learnt earlier in this unit that some legislation is already in place to protect users of ICT (for example, the Data Protection Act and the Computer Misuse Act). There are, however, other ways in which ICT may be misused, and it is these misuses that have resulted in calls for new legislative measures to be introduced.

Because the Internet can be accessed privately, people interact and behave differently online where they think their activities might go unnoticed. The issue of the Internet being 'unregulated', therefore, has, to an extent, created situations where the exchange of data and information is not welcomed by the community at large. The dangers of individuals asserting their rights to 'free speech' have been highlighted by sites that have been set up to promote criminal activities, or that encourage the dissemination of material that expresses extreme political views or is racial, pornographic or unethical in nature. Although there is only limited power to stop sites such as these being created, internet service providers have been encouraged to monitor sites that are considered to be controversial or indeed harmful to certain vulnerable sectors of the community. For example, some sites that promoted and glorified anorexia, where images of girls were displayed like trophies, have recently been closed down.

In the United States legislative procedures and the policing of sites have also led to 'raids' on individuals who have been involved with paedophilia and pornography. In addition, legislation has given the police powers to search through files and to seek out subscriber information to these sites and, if appropriate, to prosecute.

> **Think it over...**
>
> The Internet is almost like 'Jekyll and Hyde'. One part of it provides a wealth of knowledge and opportunity, freedom of expression, freedom of choice and the freedom to communicate whenever and with whom you wish. However, the other part promotes a more cynical aspect of society, a society that preys on the vulnerable and those that are easily targeted by propaganda, to be a part of racial, cultural, pornographic and illegal activities – activities that can be shared globally, with the Internet as the gateway.

The increasing power of mass lobbying will indeed bring about more changes in the legislation concerning the use of the Internet. Recently, a new law was passed in the UK to tackle the problem of 'Internet grooming' (where paedophiles surf the Web in order to lure vulnerable children into conversation). Under this new law, a paedophile was convicted in January 2005 to a four-year prison sentence. In the end, however, the Internet could be said to be about 'free speech' and the rights of individuals to 'choose', and about choices and decisions concerning what to buy, sell, view, download and whom to chat to, etc.

The information age has indeed created many opportunities for people at all levels – professionally and socially. Professionally, ICT has affected how jobs are carried out, workers' skill requirements, research and development, and the day-to-day activities of working life. Socially, ICT has enabled people to communicate better in terms of speed, interaction and creativity. People can use the Internet, messaging services, PDAs and mobile phone technology to send and receive instant text, picture and video messages. People can shop, bank and entertain from the comfort of their own home, or in transit using WAP technologies.

In terms of the impact ICT has had on social elements such as shopping, the growth in the popularity of buying online and trading through auction sites such as eBay is phenomenal (Figure 1.13).

FIGURE 1.13 *Buying and trading through eBay*

> **Knowledge check**
> * How has the Internet affected everyday communication?
> * What are the advantages and disadvantages of Internet banking?

All these elements have contributed to the growth of the digital society, a society that will continue to expand in the future.

1.4 The digital divide

Although access to ICT has transformed many people's lives in a positive way, there are also other considerations that must be addressed. As you have seen, there are people who cannot access these technologies for a variety of reasons and who therefore cannot share the digital experience.

Factors which create the digital divide

There are a number of factors that have lead to this digital divide:

* technological
* economic
* social
* geographical
* fear of technology
* lack of motivation, knowledge and skills.

Technological

Technology is advancing at an alarming rate: systems that were considered 'cutting edge' only a few years ago are now being replaced by faster, more robust systems (for example, broadband technology is rapidly replacing modems and landlines). It is no surprise, therefore, that users cannot keep up in terms of developments and costs, and so a divide has

> **Think it over...**
> What would happen if the Internet disappeared overnight? How would this affect our daily lives?

> **Assessment activity**
> How does ICT affect your daily life? Choose one particular aspect (for example, education, travel or communication) and research the impact of ICT on it.
> Include both the benefits and drawbacks of ICT. Present and compare your results with others to see the scope of the impact of ICT on our lives.

> **Assessment hint**
> ✓ Provide a description of how ICT is affecting at least five different aspects of people's lives and identify some benefits and drawbacks.
> ✓✓ Provide a description with some analysis of the benefits and drawbacks giving a clear picture of life in the information age.

📁 **Signpost for e-portfolio evidence**

Save this work in your e-portfolio. It could contribute towards covering evidence (b).

been created between those who understand and can afford these new developments and those who cannot. The digital divide has, to a large extent, been created by hardware and software manufacturers, who dictate the minimum system requirements. As new software is released, higher specification systems are needed to accommodate these.

Economic

In addition, changes in mobile phone technology and digital and satellite media mean that not only are people being forced into updating their existing provision to encompass the latest devices at a greater expense but, in some cases, the trends are also dictating what is considered to be acceptable in society. For example, peer group pressure amongst teenagers to have the latest camera or video phone has led teenagers to take drastic measures to ensure they acquire these, and thus the divide between those who can afford to keep up with the technology and those who cannot is widened even further.

There is peer group pressure amongst teenagers to have the latest mobile phone

Social

The gap is ever growing in today's society. A report commissioned by BT (see page 25) identifies how people could face social exclusion if the gap between those who have access to technology and those who do not continues to widen over the next twenty years.

This gap, however, will continue to increase if people cannot afford the costs associated with up-to-date technology. For some households, especially families, the absence of technology has in some cases made children 'social outcasts' as they cannot participate in the benefits of interactive socialising with their friends who do have access.

Geographical

Geographically, it is still impossible in some rural communities to obtain fast access to ICT – i.e. broadband connection is still not available in all parts of the country. Therefore the use of conventional dial-up methods excludes households in these areas from appreciating the full benefits of online services as the download time makes it almost impossible to tap into multimedia facilities.

Fear of technology

Some people are still wary of using technology. There are people who are happy to use a computer for the sole purpose of producing documents, etc., and nothing else, and there are others who refuse to embrace technology at all. Certain sectors of society who do not have the knowledge and, therefore, cannot access the benefits of technology remain excluded from this new information age. For more mature people, the impetus and motivation to learn about how computers work and the about the benefits they can bring are lacking. Boundaries are easily created, thus excluding them from participating in the growing digital economy.

A number of initiatives have been set up by various bodies that range from educating people about the information age to supplying low-income families with computers. However, the digital divide will only be addressed fully if there is equality in terms of every household having good access to the technology and possessing the knowledge to appreciate and engage in the services provided by the technology. This is a goal that may never be achieved because of people's differing circumstances.

Lack of motivation, knowledge and skills

The lack of skills, ability and knowledge is a reccurring issue that has contributed to the digital divide. There is a big difference in skills between those people who are competent in the use of ICT and those who are not. This has been recognised by software companies that have tried to market their software as being 'user friendly' (for example, by incorporating such features as graphical user interfaces, icons, menus and help facilities).

A user's ability or disability contributes to the digital divide. If a disabled user does not have access to the required specialist devices that can assist him or her in interfacing with a computer or other electronic device, he or she will be disadvantaged. Some of these devices include headsets and head pointers for physically disabled people or tactile keyboards that have been adapted for blind or partially sighted people.

> **Assessment activity**
>
> 1 Research three factors contributing to the digital divide. What is being done to bridge the gap?
>
> 2 Go to **www.heineman.co.uk** and use the link to Computer Aid International (express code 2008P). Learn about what the organisation does and discuss these questions:
>
> * Is it right that developing countries should get our 'cast-offs'?
> * What can they do with the equipment they are given?
> * How is their access to ICT affected by power supply and telecommunications issues?

(See Assessment hint on page 26)

CASE STUDY
The Digital Divide 2025

New report to tackle 'digital divide'

A new BT commissioned report – The Digital Divide 2025 – which the company is launching today (Tuesday) has revealed that millions of Britons could face social exclusion if the gap between those with access to technology and those without continues without direct action over the next 20 years.

Launching today at the BT Tower in London, the report – conducted by The Future Foundation – predicts that while the number of digitally excluded people will fall from 27 million to 23 million by 2025, the people excluded risk losing access to fundamental services like medical information and education.

Currently one in two adults (51 per cent) are disadvantaged by not being online and the report warns that the gap between the 'have nets' and 'have nots' will widen if the government, commercial organisations and designers of new technology fail to engage people who have so far rejected the digital age.

(Continued)

BT's corporate responsibility director Adrian Hosford said: 'Britain could be facing grave consequences if the digital divide is not taken seriously. If we don't address this problem now, it will get a lot worse. People will find it more difficult to find jobs, education opportunities will be limited and they'll simply not be able to keep up with society.

'However the good news is that there is a lot that can be done to avoid this happening. Organisations such as BT can help to tackle the problem and we have a number of grass roots projects which are working to help people in disadvantaged communities overcome digital exclusion.'

Adrian added: 'We've been working with the government and other agencies for many years now on these community projects and have already seen some wonderful results. This is a good start but more needs to be done by all those involved if we are to tackle the scale of this issue.'

BT is also a founder member of the Alliance for Digital Inclusion – an independent industry body which encourages collaboration and partnerships between industry, government and the voluntary sector to promote the use of information communication technology for social benefit.

1. Does this BT-commissioned report estimate that, by 2025, the number of digitally excluded people will increase or decrease?
2. Currently, what percentage of people are disadvantaged by not being online?
3. What consequences may be faced by Britons if the digital divide is not addressed?

Assessment hint

✓ Provide a a description of the digital divide, with some indication of the causes and effects, plus a description of two measures being taken to bridge the gap.

✓✓ Provide a description of the digital divide, with some analysis of the causes and effects, plus a description of two measures being taken to bridge the gap.

Signpost for e-portfolio evidence

Save this work in your e-portfolio. It could contribute towards covering evidence (c).

Knowledge check

* Who may not benefit from access to ICT?
* What are the factors contributing to the digital divide?

1.5 What is an e-book?

E-books are an alternative form of publishing to paper-based books. They are viewed on screen, either on a desktop PC or on a handheld system.

The simplest e-books are versions of traditional books that are made available in an online format, such as pdf. These can be read from beginning to end like any other book, although the use of bookmarks can make it easier to find particular sections easily.

However, the real value of e-books is realised when they make full use of multi-media components that cannot be used in traditional books, such as video, animations and sound.

E-books also exploit hypertext, with links between related topics, so that readers can follow lines of interest. This is especially useful for non-fiction e-books, but even fiction can be made more exciting by following alternative story lines.

E-books can be downloaded from the Internet or can easily be distributed on optical media.

> **Key term**
>
> *Hypertext* is text which contains links to related material, allowing the reader to jump from one section to another instead of having to read through in sequence.
>
> The concept of hypertext was invented in 1945, just as the first computers were being developed. It had only limited applications in, for example, computer games and paper based adventure books, until the Web was introduced in the 1990s.

> **Theory into practice**
>
> Search the Web for different examples of e-books (for example, novels, reference books, user guides, collaborative books (books written by more than one author), children's books, etc.).

Presentation of e-books

The way any written material is presented can affect the way in it is interpreted and understood. The factors that can influence an understanding of all written materials include:

* the content (i.e. the subject matter the writing discusses)
* the structure and layout (how the writing is organised into chapters, sections, etc., the number of words (or pages) it contains and the way the material is arranged on the page)
* the style of the language the author(s) have chosen to use
* its fitness for its purpose (i.e. has it been written in the most appropriate way for the intended readership?).

There are some factors, however, that apply specifically to e-books:

* their use of multimedia components
* the way the readers navigate through the e-book
* how easy or not it is to use or access.

Content

Almost any type of book can be designed and viewed as an e-book. However certain books do lend themselves more to being in an electronic format. These can include:

* encyclopaedias
* manuals and instruction books
* catalogues
* story books.

The content of an e-book is not very different to the content of a normal book. The layout may be more visually orientated with navigation aids, such as arrows, guiding you from one page to the next. Links can also be incorporated to take you to key sections within the text.

Structure and layout

There are many things that affect the way all books are structured and laid out. For example, if an organisation wanted to design an e-book that is to be used as a training manual for newly appointed staff, it might be necessary to include many different documents in this e-book that have been written by staff in all departments of that organisation. To make sure each section of the e-book covers the same points as the others (safe working practices, health and safety, etc.) and that each section is immediately recognisable, the compiler of the e-book would use templates and standard connections. This way not only would the readers understand the overall structure of the e-book but the compiler would also be able to ensure all facets of training were included.

The layout of an e-book can also be affected by the tools and techniques the author or compiler has chosen to use and by such things as the size and style of fonts:

Format, size and style of fonts

The layout will also be affected by the insertion of pictures, graphics, cartoons or photographs. These are used for a number of different purposes which range from providing a general understanding of such things as human anatomy to humour, through the insertion of cartoons and comic strips.

Pictures will enhance any e-book, providing they are used for a specific purpose. Graphs and charts can provide the readers with a visual interpretation of data shown in tables but, again, must be used for a purpose.

The number of pages in an e-book will have an impact on how easily the material is understood. For example, if all you need is a couple of pages outlining how to set up a spreadsheet, trying to master a thousand-page book on the uses and applications of software could be futile experience. Similarly, reading a few pages on surgery would not qualify you to perform surgery.

Language and style

The way in which any writing is expressed (in terms of the language it uses and its level of formality – i.e. whether it is informal and 'chatty' or formal and impersonal) will also influence the reader. Readers will have expectations that certain reading matter will be presented in a particular way. For example, you would have different expectations of:

* exam papers
* instruction manuals
* course textbooks
* letters
* legal documents.

If you picked up a romantic novel you would expect the language to be informal and familiar, and to suit the context of telling a story. A course textbook, however, would be more technical, outlining specific techniques or theories in a more formal way.

Fitness for its purpose

While all e-books should have a good balance between written and visual information, all should be written in a language and style that reflect their intended purpose and audience. The writer or compiler of an e-book must understand the needs and expectations of the readers and must arrange the material in such a way these needs and expectations are met.

Multimedia

Moving images have become one of the most important forms of visual communication, especially with the ever-increasing popularity of the Internet and mobile and digital technologies. The dynamics of an e-book allow for the use of multimedia tools and techniques, including moving images (video clips, etc.).

In an e-book, multimedia facilities can provide a more dynamic experience for the readers. Depending on its purpose, an e-book can use multimedia to:

* advertise and sell
* entertain
* instruct and educate.

The use of multimedia will transform a very static document into a dynamic, creative document that entices the readers into viewing the content.

Navigation

Navigating through an e-book is as easy as turning the pages of a normal book but with the added benefits of using links on certain key words to advance you further in the text. Similar to the navigation devices on a website, an e-book can be set up with tools to assist you in turning over the pages and advancing through the text.

> **Think it over…**
>
> When reading books printed on paper we move from one page to the next by physically turning the paper it's printed on (turning the page). How do e-books emulate this?

Ease of use and accessibility

Almost anybody can use and access an e-book; you do not need any specialist skills or software to download or view it. Once the e-book has been selected, it will download and be ready for you to navigate through, similar to a traditional textbook. The navigation buttons will guide you through each page and assist you with the selection of any command or information that you wish to view.

Evaluation of e-books

When you evaluate e-books, you should consider all those things discussed in the previous section that go to make an e-book successful or not. To do this, you should look at the layout, style, presentation and use of multimedia tools and techniques in a variety of e-books and assess these to see whether or not the e-books fulfil the purpose they set out to achieve. You should study a variety of e-books that have different purposes. For example:

- creative writing books
- reference materials (for example, encyclopaedias and historical manuscripts)
- collaborative projects (i.e. books written by more than one author)
- children's books.

Assessment activity

Design an e-book that conforms to a given technical specification.

Assessment hint

✓ Identify the content of an e-book and start to develop an e-book that demonstrates the use of suitable ready-made multimedia components, original creation, the use of appropriate software.

✓✓ Identify the content of an e-book and start to develop an e-book that demonstrates the selection and appropriate use of suitable ready-made multimedia components, creation and appropriate use of original multimedia components, the use of appropriate software and good use of testing and quality assurance procedures.

Signpost for e-portfolio evidence

Save this work in your e-portfolio. It could contribute towards covering evidence (d) and (e).

Knowledge check

1. What is an e-book?
2. What are the different stages of creating an e-book?

1.6 Developing an e-book

There are a number of things you must consider when you develop your own e-book:

- the intended audience
- the purpose of the e-book
- any content that must be included
- the message you are trying to convey
- the technical specification you must adhere to
- the deadline for completion.

Storyboards

Key term

A *storyboard* (see Figure 1.14) is a panel or a series of panels of rough sketches that can outline a sequence of events or activities in a story, normally associated with a plot or film production. A storyboard can be used in the initial stages of developing an e-book where rough ideas and designs can be sketched to form the basis of each page.

FIGURE 1.14 *An example of a storyboard*

❋ REMEMBER!

When creating a storyboard, check that the final product will meet the needs of the audience.

How to create an e-book

To start your e-book, you can draft some ideas in Word, identifying titles, content, suggested graphics, etc. Once you have generated your ideas, separate each topic onto a separate page in Word as it would appear in the order of the e-book. Each single page will form an HTML page of your e-book.

However you create your e-book, at some point you will need an e-book compiler. An e-book compiler is a program that takes the source files (the content of your e-book) and compiles them into an easy-to-distribute format.

Types of compilers

There are three main types of compilers that you could use:

* HTML compilers
* PDF compilers
* other compilers.

HTML compilers

HTML compilers convert HTML files (like those on a website) into an easy-to-distribute format, often self-contained Windows programs.

An HTML compiler may be a good choice for you if:

* you generally expect your e-book to be read on the computer screen (not all HTML e-books print well or easily).
* you want to take advantage of the 'special' features used on web pages, or that some HTML compilers allow to be used in e-books (for example: CGI forms)
* you have experience designing web pages. (Creating your e-book is likely to be a similar process to creating web pages.)

PDF compilers

PDF is a file format created by Adobe that can be used for e-books (and distributing other types of documents too).

A PDF compiler may be a good choice if any of the following apply:

* you want your e-book to be printed – PDFs print easily and well
* you want the e-book to always have an exact appearance as specified by you – PDFs look like the original document
* you do not have experience designing web pages
* you want to reach an audience who cannot read HTML compiled e-books – for example Apple Macintosh users.

If you are going to create PDF files, you will need the PDF authoring tools, the PDF file format and the software for publishing in this format.

Other compilers

There are also e-book compilers that convert other file formats such as plain text into e-books.

The template for your e-book can be pre-defined if you are using specialist design and template software, or you can create your own e-book template. If you are designing your own template, you should ensure that you include the following:

* an index page that will form the entry point to your e-book
* a contents page listing the chapters, etc.
* a link at the top of each page taking you back to the contents page
* a chapter title on the top of each page
* a set of links at the top of each page allowing you to navigate through your e-book
* forward and backward hyperlinked arrows allowing you to navigate between pages.

If you follow these steps you should find that you create a very functional and user-friendly e-book.

Development issues

When you are well on the way to developing your e-book, you should check it regularly:

* Proofread it to make sure the spelling,

punctuation and grammar are correct and that the language is appropriate for the subject matter and the readers (for example, technical language is appropriate for an e-book on computers but not for a children's story).

* Check the layout to ensure it meets the specified requirements and that it is functional (for example, can the users navigate through the pages easily?).
* Check all the links and pathways to ensure they work and that they have been integrated correctly.
* Try it out on 'test users' to ensure your e-book is functional and fit for its purpose.

To obtain constructive feedback on your e-book, you should test it on a range of end-users so that they can give you their comments. To collect this feedback, you could use a form such as that given in Table 1.3 so that all the feedback you receive covers the same areas.

> *** REMEMBER!**
>
> E-books must always fit their brief and the target audience. No matter how good a multimedia product is, there is always room for improvement!

> **Knowledge check**
>
> What factors should be considered when testing an e-book?

> *** REMEMBER!**
>
> Creating an e-book is part of your assessment for this unit. You will also need to evaluate your e-book.

Please rate this e-book by ticking a number from 1 to 5 for each of the criteria listed:

1 = excellent; 2 = very good; 3 = good; 4 = average; 5 = below average

		1	2	3	4	5
1	Content of the e-book (textual and visual)					
2	Overall structure					
3	Screen layout of the pages					
4	Use of multimedia components					
5	Presentation techniques					
6	Ease of navigation					
7	Consistency of information and layout					
8	Accessibility					
9	Suitability for the given audience					
10	Use of language/technical content					
	Any other comments and recommendations:					

TABLE 1.3 *E-book feedback form*

Evaluating your e-book

When you evaluate your e-book, you should consider how its content is set out in terms of layout, style, format and structure.

If you have followed the stages involved in creating an e-book carefully, you should find that there are no issues concerning the design, how it looks and how it works. At the end of the design, you should feel that your e-book meets all of your original objectives in terms of the content, layout and functionality. Therefore, in the evaluation part, these are the areas that you need to concentrate on.

You should evaluate each stage of the e-book design, from the original draft designs and use of Word for setting out your initial ideas, through to the compiling and template structure. The types of questions that you should be addressing in this evaluation stage include:

* Has all of the topic and content been covered fully?
* Are there any areas that have been missed out, and if so why?
* Did you manage to work within your own deadlines?
* Did you feel that you had enough knowledge and skills to develop the e-book, and how was this reflected in your final design?
* Does the e-book look professional?
* Does the e-book have a mix of graphics and text, colour and multimedia?
* Do all of the links and navigation buttons work?
* Is the e-book easy to read?

By evaluating all of these areas, you should find that you have addressed the main, layout, style, format and structure issues.

Assessment activity

An important part of any design and development is the final evaluation. Provide some evaluative comments about the key features of your e-book.

Assessment hint

✓ Provide evaluative comments about your e-book.

✓✓ Provide a detailed evaluation, incorporating feedback from test users on the key features of the e-book.

Signpost for e-portfolio evidence

Save this work in your e-portfolio. It could contribute towards covering evidence (e).

1.7 ICT skills

The Internet is one of the most dynamic research tools available – it provides a bank of information on a multitude of topics, however obscure or diverse. One of the major advantages of using the Internet to carry out research is the fact that everything can be accessed from a single computer: there is no need physically to visit different places to gather information because this is what the Internet is doing on your behalf.

Advantages of using the Internet to research

There are many advantages in using the Internet as a research tool:

* A wide range of topics and interests can be found.
* It is a concentrated source of research – there is no need for you to collect information from elsewhere.
* It is relatively quick.
* It can be a cheaper method of data collection than some other research tools (for example, you do not incur travelling and photocopying costs).
* It can be easy to use.

* Online help is provided to assist you in gathering the information.
* You do not need to depend on others to delivery the information (for example, you do not have to wait for it to arrive in the post).
* The information is presented in a variety of formats which aids your understanding and learning.
* You can receive up-to-the-minute information.
* You can share information and ideas easily through online user groups.

There are, however, problems when using the Internet as a research tool:

* You may not be familiar with its use and how to search for information.
* It can be frustrating to use a search engine for information on a such a broad topic as 'universities' because anything with 'universities' in the title will be displayed from all over the world, bringing up perhaps thousands or more sites.
* It is vital you are familiar with the way search engines work, with advanced features, Boolean operators, links and with the basics of keying in a web address. If not, you may have problems searching for appropriate and meaningful information.

Research using the Internet

When you embark on your research using the Internet, there a number of tools and techniques you can use to help in the research process.

Browser software

Browser software (Figure 1.15) enables you to move from one site to another. For example, the **Forward** and **Backward** buttons permit you to go back to the previous page or to move forward to the next. **Home** returns you to your home page, and **History** to review the pages you have visited in the past few weeks.

FIGURE 1.15 *Internet Explorer toolbar*

Sites you find that you think will be useful to you later you can add to **Favorites** (click on **Favorites, Add to Favorites**). By clicking the **Favorites** button on the toolbar, you will be able to see a list of those sites already saved in Favorites. Clicking on the **Organize...** button brings up the **Organize Favorites** dialogue box (Figure 1.16), where you can create new folders, move stored sites to other folders and delete any unwanted sites.

FIGURE 1.16 *Organize Favorites dialogue box*

Search engines

To use search engines effectively, you must be able to refine your searches, otherwise you may be presented with thousands of irrelevant sites. The search engine itself may offer you choices to limit your search (in Figure 1.17 you can limit your search to the UK only or Ireland only, instead of searching all the Web).

FIGURE 1.17 *Yahoo!'s search engine*

Other ways to refine your search include the use of logical operators (AND (or + or &), NOT (or -) and OR) between the words you enter in the search box. If you use AND (or + or &), your results should produce sites that contain all the words you joined together with AND. If you use NOT (or -), the sites shown should not contain the words that come after NOT, and if you use OR the sites should contain all or any of the words you separated with OR.

Navigation of websites

Most websites contain navigation buttons that take you to other pages on that website. In Figure 1.18, you could click on the navigation button 'IT & Office Technology', which would then bring up pages devoted to these books.

> **Theory into practice**
>
> Visit this website http://www.train-ed.co.uk and practise your navigation skills and your browser options.

Hyperlinks

Some sites have hyperlinks to other sites that may contain information that could be of value to you. In Figure 1.18, if you were to click on 'Heinemann Direct', you would be taken to the site shown in Figure 1.19.

FIGURE 1.19 *Hyperlinks take you to related sites*

Judging the quality of the information found

Once you have found a site that seems to provide the information you need, you must make an informed judgement about its accuracy, reliability and currency.

FIGURE 1.18 *Navigation buttons*

Theory into practice

Using the Internet as a research tool, carry out searches on the following subjects and record the information you obtain using a template such as the one provided in Table 1.4. You should use four search engines to undertake this activity.

Find out information on:

1. The five latest cinema film releases
2. An actor or actress who appears in two new film releases
3. What other films this actor or actress has appeared in.

When you have finished your searches, present a summary of the information you have obtained to the rest of your group. You should use an appropriate software tool to deliver this information, such as PowerPoint.

Acknowledgements

If you decide to use information you find on a website, you must acknowledge the fact that this was the source of the information – you must not attempt to masquerade the information as your own. This is plagiarism – passing information off as your own when you have in fact copied it from elsewhere.

Think it over...

There are a number of ways that people would expect you to acknowledge any information that you have used from their website. These can include:

* E-mailing or writing off for permissions.
* Acknowledging the author/company in your work or on your website.
* Providing a link on your website to their website (if appropriate).

Have a look at a range of websites, for example, media, forum sites, sporting sites, major companies, etc., and see whether or not you can use materials from their site, and what you need to do in order to download, copy and paste it.

Multimedia content for e-books

One of the most important features of all e-books is that they contain images and links. It is this that differentiates e-books from normal, static textbooks and makes them more dynamic to read. To make sure the e-books you create are dynamic, there are a number of steps you can follow:

1. Try to use ready-made multimedia components.
2. Use a digital camera and scanner to capture images.
3. Try to capture screen-based images.
4. Use word-processed documents.
5. Create links.
6. Use appropriate file formats.
7. Try to combine information created in one type of software with information created in a different type of software.

Search engine:	Web page address:
Links used:	
Summary of site information:	

TABLE 1.4 *Internet research template*

Theory into practice

Research ready-made multimedia components. Write up your report and save in your e-portfolio.

Signpost for e-portfolio evidence

Save this work in your e-portfolio. It could contribute towards covering evidence (d), (e) and (f).

UNIT ASSESSMENT

1. Using your experience of creating an e-book, write up your report and include:
   * what design principles you followed and why
   * who was your intended audience and did your audience affect specific elements of your e-book (i.e. size of text, etc)?
2. From your evaluation of your e-book, what would you do to improve it?

UNIT 2

The digital economy

Introduction

This unit is about how the Internet has transformed the way business is done. ICT has always had an important role in supporting the information needs of organisations and, with the advent of the World Wide Web, transactions that are entirely electronic have become a reality. This unit builds on the material covered in Unit 1, so you should have completed that unit before you start this one.

What you need to learn

In completing this unit, you should achieve these learning outcomes:

* Know about the different information needs of organisations
* Understand the advantages and disadvantages of shopping online
* Have investigated the design of commercial transactional websites
* Be able to describe the back-office processes associated with making an online purchase
* Create and use a database to store a set of data and extract meaningful information from it, or order it to identify significant patterns and trends and make recommendations.

Resource toolkit

To complete this unit, you need these essential resources:

* access to computer hardware, including a printer
* access to computer software, in particular database software such as Microsoft Access®
* access to the Internet.

How you will be assessed

This unit is internally assessed. Page vii explains what this means.

There are four assessment objectives:

AO1 Investigate the design of a commercial transactional website.

AO2 Use diagrams to show what happens when someone purchases a product online.

AO3 Investigate potential threats to customer data collected via the Web and the measures taken to protect it.

AO4 Create a database to store a given set of data and extract useful information from it and evaluate it.

To demonstrate your coverage of these assessment objectives, you will produce an e-portfolio of evidence, showing what you have learnt and what you can do:

(a) You will write a description of the design of a commercial transactional website, including details of its structure, the goods offered, the way customer information is captured and payments are made, and the techniques used to engage and retain customers. This will also include an in-depth evaluation of the key features of the website design and some suggestions for improvements.

(b) You will include detailed diagrams illustrating the chain of events involved in an online purchase, showing information flows and the back-office processes.

(c) You will write a description and evaluation of the security and legislation issues relevant to online selling.

(d) You will create a customised database designed to store a given set of data, and provide recommendations based on the trends identified from the given data.

(e) You will provide an evaluation of your own performance on this unit.

How high can you aim?

Your e-portfolio will contain all the evidence on which your performance will be judged. Some **Assessment activities** can be used towards your e-portfolio. These contain **Assessment hints** on what you can do to pass (✓), gain a better mark (✓✓) or top marks (✓✓✓). For example, when describing the design of a commercial transactional website you can only obtain the higher marks if your description includes an in-depth evaluation of the techniques used to engage, retain and/or entice the customers, and an evaluation of the site as a whole and the 'customer experience' it provides. You should also make suggestions for improvements.

The diagrams you draw to explain the process of placing an online order should describe the back-office processes in detail (payment processing, stock control, despatch, etc.), as well as the processes involving direct interaction with the customer.

In the section on security threats, preventative measures and legislation, you need to provide in-depth evaluations as well as descriptions of these aspects of e-commerce to achieve the higher marks.

The database you create must include appropriate fields types, formats and validation checks and you need to carry out sorts and searches on the data you import into the database and present the results in a clear, easy-to-understand format. Finally, you must interpret the output from the sorts and searches you do on the given dataset, and the degree to which you can identify significant trends and make recommendations for future developments will determine your mark.

> **Ready to start?**

Why not keep a log of the time you take to complete this unit? Devise a blank form that you could use to record the time that you spend on this course.

2.1 Information needs of organisations

Information is, in many ways, the life blood of most organisations. This is nothing new, but the use of ICT has revolutionised how information is gathered, communicated and analysed. Since the 1950s computers have been used by organisations to support their information processing needs, so that today all but the very smallest of businesses are heavily reliant on ICT. Since the 1980s another revolution has taken place – the phenomenal growth of the Internet – which has provided a completely new way for organisations to communicate with their customers and each other.

Not all organisations are the same, and different organisations have different information needs. There are a number of ways to categorise organisations. Dividing them into public and private sectors is one way to do this, which is useful because organisations in these different sectors have different priorities and therefore different information requirements:

* *Public sector* organisations are funded by the public through taxes and they provide some kind of service to the public. As such they are ultimately controlled by the government and are accountable to them and the public. Examples include schools, libraries, local councils, the police and the armed forces.
* *Private sector* organisations are owned by individuals or shareholders and range from self-employed people to large multinational corporations such as Ford, Sony and Tesco.

Another way organisations can be classified is by their type. Just as organisations in different sectors have different information requirements, so different types of organisations use ICT for different things. Companies generally fall into one of three categories, industrial, commercial and service:

* *Industrial* – companies that either manufacture things or produce the raw materials (such as oil, iron, copper) from which things are made. Examples in this sector are Shell, the Ford Motor Company and British Aerospace. The key uses for ICT in industrial organisations include the control of manufacturing processes, the research, design and development of new products, and the control of the stock of components from which finished goods are made.

> **Key terms**
>
> *Stock* is the goods that a company has in storage which, in the case of a commercial organisation, is waiting to be sold. The items on the shelves of a supermarket are also stock. *Stock control* refers to the methods an organisation uses to track and record the stock it has. Stock costs money to buy and so is a valuable asset. Keeping just the right amount of stock is also important: too much stock is a waste of money, too little may leave customers dissatisfied.

* *Commercial* – companies sell the goods that the industrial organisations make. Examples include Sainsbury's, Argos and your local corner shop. Commercial companies use ICT systems for the control of purchasing, stock control and the recording of sales transactions.

> **Key term**
>
> A *transaction* is an agreement to provide goods or services in exchange for payment. A simple transaction could just be buying a packet of sweets from a corner shop; more complex transactions can involve negotiations on things such as price, payment terms and delivery dates.

* *Service* – companies provide a service, either to other businesses or to people like you. Banks and insurance companies are examples of these types of organisations. Most public sector organisations fall into this category. The key uses for ICT include keeping track of customer accounts and transactions.

The vast majority of the organisations you come into contact with on a day-to-day basis are in the commercial or service sector. The customers for many commercial organisations such as shops and supermarkets are people like you and I. However, these commercial organisations are customers in their own right. The goods they sell have to be made by other organisations, so an electrical store such as Comet is a customer of an industrial organisations such as Sony or Hotpoint. These industrial companies are in turn customers of the companies that make components such as electric motors or switches from which their finished goods are made. Most businesses therefore have a complex series of customer and supplier relationships.

In what ways do these different organisations use ICT to communicate and do business? The following examples briefly explain how ICT can be used to support key business processes.

Capturing and processing data

Many organisations – from schools and colleges to banks, utility companies and supermarkets – need to capture and process large quantities of data. This data capture was originally done via the computer's keyboard. Organisations such as banks and utility companies (gas, electricity, water and other service suppliers) have to record a large amount of data from:

* customers' cheques (in the case of banks)
* meter readings (in the case of gas and electricity suppliers).

These companies employed what are called data-entry clerks to carry out this task. Technology has since developed easier ways to capture data than through the keyboard. Personal cheques have been largely replaced by credit and debit cards which contain a magnetic strip that can be read by magnetic card reader. The data entry is therefore done via a credit card terminal in the shop. Gas and electricity meter readers no longer write the meter readings down on a form; instead they use a hand-held computer and enter the data on site. The data from the hand-held computer is then downloaded into the utility company's computer when the meter reader returns to his or her office at the end of the day.

Bar codes are another example of how technology has made data capture possible. Prior to its use, shops and supermarkets had no easy way to capture sales information. But now, since almost every item in a shop has a bar code which can be simply and quickly read by a bar code scanner, item prices can be stored (and easily modified) on the shop's computer. As items are sold the shop's stock records can also be updated, making stock control and the reordering of goods an automated process.

Bar codes have made the electronic capture of data possible

> **Key term**
>
> A *bar code* is a internationally recognised, machine-readable symbol. Bar codes are made up of vertical black stripes of different widths. The different widths of the stripes represent different numbers, so a product number can be coded into a bar code. Bar codes can be read by a scanning device which passes a beam of light over the bar code. The width of the bars are detected by the device, which measures how much light is reflected from the bar code, and this information is converted back into a number. Bar codes are widely used in a number of applications where items need to be recognised, such as supermarkets, stock control and asset management.

Presenting and exchanging information

Originally conceived as calculating machines, it wasn't long before the usefulness of computers was greatly enhanced by their being able to communicate the information they stored and processed. The World Wide Web itself was originally created to enable scientists to communicate and share the results of their research. Email has become the method of business communication, largely replacing the paper-based letter and memo. As well as sending text, email attachments can consist of pictures, music, documents and any machine-readable file. Other methods of computer communication include videoconferencing and online 'chat', where users can interact with each other in real time. All these methods of communication are used both for business and pleasure.

Conducting transactions

As we have already discussed, businesses are often involved in a complex series of customer and supplier relationships. Many large commercial and industrial organisations purchase large quantities of goods from a wide range of different suppliers. Supermarkets, for example, stock tens of thousands of items on their shelves, purchased from thousands of different suppliers. Motor car manufacturers also purchase many thousands of different components, ranging from nuts and bolts to tyres and radios.

Managing the purchase of these different items is a major task, and these transactions between buyer and supplier have also been revolutionised by ICT. Businesses that used to exchange order forms, invoices and other paper documents now complete their transactions electronically using EDI (electronic data interchange). The general public now rarely use a

> **Key terms**
>
> *Video conferencing* is a communication technique using audio and video links to allow remote groups of people to have a 'virtual' meeting. Connections can be made using computers over the Internet, although the quality of the video can be poor if the link speed is low. Video conferencing has obvious benefits for business meetings in that it saves the time and expense involved in travelling.
>
> *Real time* is a term which refers to events that take place more or less immediately. Internet chat rooms, for example, allow users to exchange messages with only few seconds' delay. Email, on the other hand, does not take place in real time. Emails are transferred to a recipient's server and are only downloaded when the user logs on (this is sometimes called 'store and forward'). Therefore users must be online simultaneously to communicate using real-time methods, but need not both be online at the same time to communicate using email.

> **Key term**
>
> *Electronic data interchange (EDI)* is a method used by businesses to transfer documents electronically. In the past, businesses carried out transactions by sending and receiving many paper documents, such as order forms, invoices, etc. EDI allows these transactions to be completed electronically over the Internet or other network.

written cheque to pay for goods as credit and debit cards allow the transaction to be electronically authorised and recorded in real time. Although cash still remains popular for many transactions, that, too, may one day be replaced by a form of electronic money.

Marketing goods and services

ICT has not traditionally been used to market a company's goods and services. Radio, TV, billboard and newspaper advertising have been the media that have been most commonly used. However, the popularity of the Internet has meant that many companies, both large and small, have websites that provide information about their goods and services. While websites are still not the primary means of advertising for most companies, many companies direct interest to their websites from more direct forms of advertising. Website information is much easier and cheaper to update and add to than information contained in traditional sales leaflets and brochures. Websites can also include such media as sound, animation and video which cannot be included in leaflets and brochures. It is now unusual, therefore, to see an advert that does not suggest people should look up the company's website for more information.

Distributing goods

Commercial organisations (such as supermarkets) have a large number of stores, all of which need to be kept stocked with a huge variety of goods. It is a major task to plan and control the distribution of these goods to the stores in a timely and efficient manner. They also have to bear in mind that many of the goods may be perishable, so they need to be delivered to stores promptly. Computerised distribution systems control the movement of goods inside large regional distribution centres, ensuring the correct goods are loaded on to the correct lorry in the correct order. These systems not only ensure the correct goods are loaded for each store but also plan the route the delivery lorry will take to ensure the most efficient use of time and fuel.

Managing customer relations

The rise of the 'call centre' is another recent phenomenon which relies heavily on ICT. Many large organisations now provide customers with a central enquires telephone number which will connect customers to a computer-controlled telephone-response system. Some enquiries may be dealt with without human operator involvement. For example, in many cases bank customers can listen to their current account balance or make payments using an automated menu system with input from the customer via his or her telephone keypad.

For enquiries that cannot be dealt with by automated systems, customers may be routed to human operators. These operators, in order to reduce labour costs, may be situated across the globe, with many Asian countries being popular locations for call centre staff. Call centre staff use computers to access customer details and their purchasing or other transaction histories so that they can answer customer queries and resolve problems. Specialised customer relationship management software (often referred to by its initials, CRM) is often used to record details of customers' queries so that call centre staff can see the history of a query even though they may not have previously spoken to the customer.

Managing customer relationships is an important activity that, in the past, relied on personal contact. However, ICT has provided a number of cost-effective alternatives. Many organisations direct their customers to their websites for help and support, providing facilities such as FAQs (frequently asked questions) to deal with common problems, and email contact or support forms for more individual problems.

> **Think it over...**
>
> What are the benefits and drawbacks (both to the customer and the organisation) of locating call centres in remote locations?

Optimising just-in-time purchasing of stock and components

Manufacturing organisations that purchase large amounts of stock to be used in the manufacturing process often implement so-called 'just-in-time' (or JIT) manufacturing systems. Just-in-time systems aim to deliver components only as they are needed in the manufacturing process, thereby reducing the stock that has to be held in the warehouse. JIT techniques benefit from the use of ICT because they allow organisations to:

* keep accurate records of components kept in stock
* keep a close control on the manufacturing process so that the timing and quantities of required components can be monitored
* communicate electronically with suppliers so that orders can be placed promptly.

It's difficult to think of an area of business that has not been affected, if not revolutionised, by the computer. Even prior to the World Wide Web, computers had a profound effect on the way businesses operate, but since its explosive growth that revolution has spread out of the office and factory and has begun to change the way people sell goods and services.

> **Knowledge check**
>
> Select an organisation from each of the categories listed earlier (public, commercial, industrial) and list the different ways they use ICT to collect and process information.

2.2 From 'brick' to 'click'

Traditionally, those organisations that sell products or services have done so by one of two methods:

* a high-street shop, with customers visiting the shop and buying the goods in person
* mail order, with customers selecting goods via a printed catalogue and having them delivered.

With the advent of the Internet, online shopping has become possible. Online selling does not require a physical presence: traditional methods of selling took the form of the 'bricks and mortar' of the high-street shop or, in the case of mail-order selling, the paper catalogue and the telesales person at the end of a phone line. The term 'virtual' is often used to describe online selling since it has, or appears to have, no physical presence.

> **Key term**
>
> *Virtual* has become a commonly used term in the realm of computing and the Internet. The term literally means 'having the effect but not the physical presence'. So a virtual-reality computer game has the effect of being on a battlefield without you actually physically being there. The Internet, therefore, provides you with a 'virtual shopping mall' with all the features of a shopping mall but without you actually being in one.

The explosion in the growth of the Internet in the 1990s created sufficient online users for technically minded entrepreneurs to consider setting up online stores. Most of these were initially in the United States, but they soon spread to Europe and other countries where Internet usage is high. Online retailers, such as the bookseller, Amazon, were amongst the first to set up sites in the United States and Europe.

Setting up an online store

What is required to set up an Internet store? Many of the ingredients are similar to those needed for a traditional store, but there are some important differences:

* You must have a product or service to offer.
* You need a way to encourage buyers to visit your store, which is known as marketing. This is more difficult than with traditional stores since an Internet store has no physical presence and, therefore, without any marketing, no one will know the site is there. An important part of any online store's marketing is its domain name

CASE STUDY

The dot com 'bubble'

In the late 1990s, entrepreneurs and financiers became aware of the Internet and the potential that online selling held. Many people thought the Internet would become the 'next big thing' and that those who got in early and set up e-commerce sites would make large amounts of money. This was something like the 'goldrush' that occurred in America in the nineteenth century. Financiers lent these people millions of pounds to set up websites, and companies like lastminute.com were valued very highly, with their founders apparently being worth millions.

One of the websites set up at this time was boo.com. This online fashion clothing store was set up by three Swedish entrepreneurs and quickly attracted over £80 million in funding. They had an ambitious plan for a stylish and sophisticated website, which sold to 18 different European countries. However, technical problems meant that the site took a long time to develop and, when it was launched in November 1999, the problems did not stop. The extensive use of graphics, 3D images and pop-up windows made the site very slow to download and frustrating to use. At that time only around 1 per cent of Internet users in Europe had a broadband link. The site also required the Macromedia Flash browser plug-in to work properly but, at that time, few people had this plug-in. People who tried the site found their bad experiences off-putting, and even though boo.com modified its site, many users did not return. The company was forced to close down only six months after it was launched, due to lack of funds (the company had spent the £80 million it raised!) and its inability to raise any more money.

The collapse of boo.com and a number of other dot.com companies scared investors and the 'Internet goldrush' came to an end. The high values placed on some companies nose-dived (for example, shares in lastminute.com went from £5 per share to 20p). Lastminute, unlike boo.com, survived the dot.com boom, but only became profitable in 2003.

How are 'dot com' companies doing today? You can find lots of up-to-date articles on the fortunes of companies like Lastminute, Amazon, eBay and others on the BBC News website, which has a section dedicated to e-commerce on its business pages.

---

or web address. An easy-to-remember address is important to make it easy for customers to find the site. Web addresses are unique: their use is controlled by a central authority, and new businesses in online shopping will have difficulty finding a memorable web address that has not already been registered.

* You need a way to accept orders. A transactional website must be designed and built.
* You need a way to accept money. Accepting cash or cheques for goods purchased over the Internet is not practical, so you need to accept credit or debit cards.
* You will need a way of delivering the goods or services you sell, which is known as 'fulfilment'. With traditional stores, fulfilment is easy: the customer picks up the goods when he or she buys them. With an Internet store, unless the goods or services can be delivered electronically, they must be physically delivered, by post or courier.
* Since customers may not like what they buy, or the goods may be faulty, you will need a way to return goods. As customers cannot physically see the goods on an online site, this aspect is more important than with a traditional store. Customers will expect a guarantee that they can return the goods if they don't like them before they will buy from an Internet store.
* You will need a customer service department to help customers with problems, both technical (i.e. with the product they have bought) and with the purchasing process (i.e. with the website).

> **Key terms**
>
> A *transactional website* is a site were visitors can complete some kind of transaction. The most common type is sites were visitors can order and pay for goods (such as books or computers) or services (such as airline flights). Other types of transactional website include sites provided by banks, where customers can check their account balance, transfer money and pay bills.
>
> A *debit card* is issued by your bank and allows to you to make payments from your bank account to anyone who can accept your card. The payments are taken more or less immediately from your bank account.
>
> *Credit cards* are slightly different. With a credit card you have an account separate from your normal bank account. Purchases you make with the card are added to your account and, at the end of the month, you are sent a statement, listing all your transactions. You can pay some or all of the outstanding balance. The use of stolen credit and debit cards to obtain goods fraudulently has become a major problem.
>
> *Chip and pin* cards have been introduced to combat this. With these cards, rather than using a customer signature (which can easily be forged) to validate the card, the customer enters a PIN code into the credit card terminal in the shop though not online.

Why has online shopping proved so popular?

To understand this we need to consider the advantages both to the seller and the buyer. From the seller's perspective, there are a number of important benefits to selling online.

Access to a worldwide customer base

Traditionally, to achieve a wide geographic coverage, an organisation would need a large number of outlets spread across the country. With online selling such a coverage can be achieved without a large investment in buildings and the people to staff them. Because, in most cases, goods have to be delivered to the customers and trading laws are different in different countries, most websites only sell within the country they are located in. Companies that have a international online presence, such as Amazon and eBay, have separate sites for each country they operate in.

Low set-up and running costs

Online selling has much lower costs that traditional selling methods. The operation can be run from a single, low-cost location rather than having to pay for a large number of shops in high-cost, high-street locations. As well as the reduction in cost associated with premises, there is a very significant reduction in the labour costs. Traditional selling through shops or mail order requires shopfloor or telesales personnel, but selling via a website does not require sales personnel. The customers themselves (via the website) select and pay for the goods.

Extension of product range

Once the infrastructure of an Internet shopping site has been set up, it is relatively easy to extend the range of goods that are sold. Certain goods are ideal for selling over the Internet (for example, goods that are relatively small and light in weight will not be expensive to deliver). The Amazon website provides a good example of an organisation that, over time, has extended its product range. Originally, Amazon just sold books, but it now also sells electronic goods (digital cameras, computer accessories, etc.), music CDs, videos and DVDs, games and computer software. Amazon also sells some Internet-specific goods, such as e-books.

> **Key term**
>
> *E-books* are not paper books but digital versions of books which can be instantly downloaded from a website (see Unit 1).

Amazon has also added what it calls 'Marketplace', a concept that is unique to

Internet selling. Amazon Marketplace allows customers to sell second-hand books and other goods on the site, alongside the new goods. Customers therefore have a choice of purchasing either new or second-hand items. Amazon makes money from their Marketplace concept by charging the seller a commission on every sale they make.

Many sites, especially those selling travel products, have partnerships with sites that sell related services, so most airline websites have partnerships with sites selling car hire, hotel bookings and other related services. This is convenient both for the customer, since he or she can book his or her flight and car hire at the same time, and for the primary seller, as they receive commission from these 'follow-on' sales.

Twenty-four hour opening

Modern lifestyles often do not fit with traditional shop-opening hours: people want to be able to shop at all hours but it is often not economic to open traditional shops late at night since the numbers of customers may be quite low. Also, in the UK, Sunday opening hours are currently restricted. No such problems face online selling, which can be open 24 hours, 365 days a year at no additional cost, thus maximising the opportunity to sell goods.

Faster response times

Online shops do not have queues and there is no waiting to be served. This, on top of all the other time savings involved, such as travelling time, makes online shopping a seemingly more 'instant' experience.

Real-time sales information

There is nothing more frustrating than setting off to the local shops or to the out-of-town shopping centre in search of a particular item only to find that none of the shops has it in stock. This is not a problem with online buying. Most Internet shops provide real-time stock level information so that you can see if the item you require is available and, if it is not, many sites will give an estimated delivery date. If the site you normally use does not have the item, it is also easy to search for other sites that sell the item.

Customer expectation

Many customers expect large organisations to have an online presence and, in some cases, an online presence can complement physical stores. Buyers can do their research online in prices, specifications and such like but may decide they want to see the actual goods in store before purchasing. Or they may decide they don't want to wait for delivery, so the journey to the shop is worth the effort. Many organisations go to considerable efforts to project a good image of themselves to their customers.

A survey carried out by BT in 2004 of businesses in Britain and Germany showed that many businesses had created an e-commerce site mainly to make the company look modern and forward-looking in the eyes of their customers.

There are also many advantages to the customer:

* The ability to access a wide range of goods and services from the comfort of your home at any time of night or day is clearly a major benefit.
* Price comparisons are much easier to make online – you do not have to travel to different shops. Websites exist that will carry out price comparisons for the customer (such as those at **kelkoo.co.uk**; a link is available at www.heinemann.co.uk/hotlinks (express code 2008P)). While this is clearly an advantage to the customer, it does mean that sellers must be very price competitive, which can cut profit margins.

Disadvantages of Internet shopping

Internet shopping has many advantages for both the seller and the buyer. However, there are some important drawbacks.

Security

Probably the greatest concern for most people shopping online is security. Passing personal and financial information over the Internet poses a risk but, in many cases, the risks are exaggerated. According to Forrester research, for every £1,000 spent online, £1 is lost in fraud (this compares to £25 lost in off-line sales). None the less, there have been some high-profile errors involving online selling sites – the disclosure of credit card details, for example. In November 2004 a security loophole was identified in the Cahoot Internet Bank website. A customer discovered a way to view other people's account details, and provided details of the flaw to the BBC. The site was closed for 10 hours while the problem was resolved.

For the seller themselves, security is a headache as they must be constantly on their guard against attacks from hackers, who may try to steal customer details, and from people who are trying to obtain goods fraudulently.

Competition

The Internet shopping market can be very price competitive. People who shop via the Internet often know the product they want and are trying to find it at the lowest price. In many market areas there are a number of sites selling those products (for example, electrical and electronic goods, computers and accessories, travel) so competition is fierce, and a number of online shopping sites have failed. Internet-only sellers also face strong competition from traditional companies that have also set up websites (Argos, Comet, Tesco, etc.). These traditional companies have a well-known name, a reputation and greater marketing muscle than most Internet-only organisations.

Cannot physically see or try the goods

For certain types of goods, not being able to see or try the goods is not a problem, especially if the buyer knows exactly what he or she wants. With other goods (for example, clothes), people may prefer to see and try on the actual goods before purchasing.

Goods must be delivered

Physical goods purchased over the Internet must, of course, be delivered. This adds to the cost (especially for large or heavy goods) and means that the customer cannot have the goods immediately. Delivery can cause problems because many companies require goods to be signed for when they are delivered as a protection against fraud, especially if they are high-value items. This means customers may have to stay at home or arrange for someone to be at home to receive the goods.

The year 2004, and in particular the Christmas period, was the turning point for online retailers: a survey of shoppers that year showed that 44 per cent planned to make online purchases, compared with 21 per cent in 2003, and they were predicted to spend around £4 billion during the Christmas period, an increase of over 60 per cent on the previous year.

> **Theory into practice**
>
> Magazines, newspapers and websites such as the BBC News site have plenty of articles about the latest e-commerce issues. Reading these articles can help to develop your knowledge and understanding of the issues affecting this area.

2.3 Transactional websites

Websites that can be used to buy or sell goods or services are sometimes called transactional websites (see earlier in this unit) since they allow some kind of transaction to take place. These types of website should not be confused with the many websites which simply provide information. Transactional websites can be broadly divided into three categories. Sites which sell:

* physical goods, such as books or TV sets
* services, such as airline flights or insurance
* products that can be downloaded directly from the site, such as music and computer software.

CASE STUDY

The music industry

No other industry has been as dramatically affected by the rise of the Internet as the music industry. Since the invention of a cheap and simple audio recording system in the form of the audio cassette, the industry has faced the problem of the illegal copying of music. With the Internet the problem became a very serious one. Two other developments went along with the Internet in making large-scale music piracy practical. One was the MP3 digital music file format. This allowed digital music to be compressed into files which could be downloaded in minutes rather than hours while retaining good-quality playback. The other was peer-to-peer file sharing over the Internet. This allows users to share each other's collections of digital music directly from their own computers, rather than storing the files on a central server. These three ideas were brought together in 1999 by an 18-year-old called Shawn Fanning. He created a program which allowed searching and peer-to-peer file sharing of music files and he called it Napster.

Napster quickly became very popular since it provided a way for people to obtain music without paying for it. However, it was not popular with the music industry because it enabled people to obtain thousands of copyrighted songs without paying any royalty fee. The music industry fought for years to close down Napster, and eventually succeeded in May 2002 after a long legal battle. The illegal copying of music is still possible: a number of other peer-to-peer file-sharing programs exist, which, unlike Napster, do not maintain a central index server which lists all the users (it does not store the songs themselves), and which are therefore much harder for the music industry to find and close down.

Until quite recently no organisation had successfully set up a legal MP3 download site, where songs are available with the agreement of the music company that owns them and that can be downloaded for a fee. This was the result of the difficulty of obtaining the permission of a cautious music industry who were nervous about this new technology, and the ease with which music could be illegally obtained without charge. However, the music industry knew something had to be done because, during 2003–4, sales of legal CDs fell in some markets by as much as 30 per cent. In 2003 the music industry launched a worldwide crackdown on Internet music swapping and began to sue individuals who made large catalogues of music available over the Internet.

In May 2003, Apple computer launched the first successful legal music download site, called iTunes. Apple managed to persuade the music industry to give them permission to sell their songs, and the site linked with the enormously successful Apple MP3 player, the iPod. The iPod is stylish and sophisticated, and its success has transformed the fortunes of the Apple company, with more than 3 million iPods sold in 2004, giving Apple 50 per cent of the MP3 player market and boosting the company's profits by 50 per cent.

The iPod is stylish and sophisticated

Continued...

The iTunes site sells single songs for around 90p each, and it has sold more than 100 million songs, with 70 per cent of the market share in legal downloads. The iTunes site is a little different from many other successful e-commerce sites. Apple is a computer company, not a music company, and, unlike many sites, the product is delivered instantly and electronically over the Internet.

Napster has recently been re-launched, this time as a legal music download site, where music must be paid for.

The success of the iTunes site was partly linked to the success for the iPod player, but what other factors help the site to succeed?

You need to study such sites and, as you do so, you need to consider the following:

* the purpose of the site and how successfully it meets this objective
* how it is structured
* the goods and/or services it offers
* the product information provided
* the types of transactions that can be made and how easy it is to do so
* the methods used to capture customer information (both overt and covert) and to authenticate the identity of customers
* the techniques used to engage, retain and entice customers
* its usability and accessibility
* the 'customer experience' it offers.

In this section we will look at a number of sites to see how they address the above issues.

The purpose of the site and how it is structured

Most transactional websites which sell physical goods take the purchaser through a number of stages.

Product search, selection and information

This stage allows the customer to search for the item he or she requires, perhaps by type or name. Customers can view details of the product, and some sites show additional information about the product, such as customer reviews, etc. Figure 2.1 shows the front page of the Heinemann FE and vocational website. The name of a book (or qualification) can be entered in the Search box on the top right and this will produce a list of books that match the criteria entered.

More powerful search facilities need to be provided on sites that sell items such as holidays or airline flights as there are more criteria which need to be set. Figure 2.2 shows the home page of the British Midland Airways company, which is called flybmi.com.

The results of the search are then displayed, allowing the user to select the most suitable one. Figure 2.3 shows the search results page of the flybmi.com website, with a number of different flights to the chosen destination on the days selected. The page lists them with an **Option** button next to each.

Having searched for and found the required product, the site may provide more information about the item. The Heinemann site, for example, gives a brief description of the book, allows you to read some reviews and gives you a preview of some sample material from the book (see Figure 2.4). This page also has a link to additional items which may be relevant, such as teacher resources.

Virtual shopping basket

This allows customers to select the goods they wish to purchase and to make a list of these items. The customer can then either continue shopping and add additional items to the basket or move to the checkout. The Heinemann website has a button on the right site of the product details page

FIGURE 2.1 *Heinemann FE and vocational website*

FIGURE 2.2 *flybmi.com web page*

FIGURE 2.3 *flybmi.com search results*

FIGURE 2.4 *Product details page, Heinemann website*

(labelled **Buy now**), which will add the currently displayed item to the basket. Clicking this button adds the product and displays the basket's contents, as shown in Figure 2.5.

The shopping basket page usually has facilities to remove or modify the quantities of items previously added (the **Delete** link on the Heinemann page allows items to be removed).

Travel websites often do not have a shopping basket concept since most people only buy one flight or holiday at a time. The flybmi.com website is an example of this: once the flights (outward and, if required, return) have been chosen, a summary page is shown, with no facility to add more flights, as shown in Figure 2.6.

Types of transaction and customer registration

Checkout

Once the customer has finished shopping, he or she needs to pay for his or her goods. The transaction stage requires that the customer is registered with the site. Customers who are already registered can enter their authentication details and confirm the delivery address and payment details. Customers who are not registered must go through the registration stage.

Registration

This stage involves the customer providing his or her personal details, including delivery address, email address and payment details in the form of the credit or debit card number, security code and expiry date. Figure 2.7 shows the customer registration page from the Heinemann site.

Confirmation

Having registered, the customer's credit card details will be validated and authorisation for the sale obtained from his or her credit card company. The final stage in the process is the display of the confirmation page, which gives details of the purchase that has been made.

FIGURE 2.5 *Heinemann website shopping basket*

FIGURE 2.6 *The flybmi.com summary page*

FIGURE 2.7 *Customer registration on the Heinemann website*

Confirmation is normally also sent to the customer's email address. An order or booking reference code is also usually issued. This can be used if there is any query about the order or, in the case of the flight, it is used at the airport check-in to identify the customer's flight booking.

Airline tickets and books are, of course, not the only things you can buy online, but most sites follow the same structure. For example, another popular type of transaction website is online banking. Most traditional banks allow customers to access their account details online and provide facilities for them to view their statements, to transfer money and to pay bills. An number of Internet-only banks have also sprung up. The key benefit of online banking is convenience, but security is a major headache (see the section on security page 47).

The two transactional websites described here (flybmi and Heinemann) are fairly typical, but there are many more examples. Most follow a similar layout but there are differences between them. Many sites provide more sophisticated facilities to assist the purchaser in making his or her choices. Some sites also encourage the customer to purchase related items. Amazon, for example, features lists of additional items that people who bought a particular product also purchased. Sites which sell computer hardware and electronic goods also often feature lists of related items or accessories that can be used with the items chosen.

Attracting customers

Transactional websites use a variety of techniques to encourage customers to spend time on their sites, visit them regularly and purchase items. Large sums of money are spent on designing and developing a visually interesting site with images and animations that encourage users to visit and explore it. Sites also need to be updated regularly to maintain the interest of returning customers.

Sites attempt to retain existing customers in a number of ways. Personalised offers and suggested purchases is one way this can be done and most sites will send registered customers regular e-mails reminding them of special offers and the latest products.

The site's usability and accessibility

No one likes using a site that is slow, keeps crashing or is difficult to use. This was one of the

CASE STUDY

eBay

eBay is something of an Internet phenomenon. The site has been enormously successful with versions in 29 different countries and profits of over $182 million in the three months to the end of September 2004. eBay has been likened to an online car-boot sale: unlike the sites we have discussed so far, eBay does not sell its own products; instead, anyone can auction his or her goods on the site. With something like 25 million items for sale at one time, eBay has 114 million registered users worldwide, with 8.7 million in the UK alone. Items up for auction include anything from a Gulf Stream jet aircraft (sold for £2.57 million – the most expensive so far) to cars, jewellery, computer goods and antiques.

eBay was founded in 1997 by an American called Pierre Omidyar who wanted a way for his wife to trade her collection of Pez dispensers (Pez is an American sweet that comes in different styles of plastic dispensers).

eBay makes its money from the commission charged to people who sell their goods on the site; it does not handle, stock or ship the goods – it's down to the sellers to do that.

1. What is it that makes eBay so successful?
2. What benefits for the company that runs the site does eBay have over more traditional e-commerce sites?

major problems with the boo.com site mentioned earlier. Site designers need to strike a delicate balance between making the site interesting and making it too complex. The site design needs to be intuitive so that it is obvious to users how to use it and they don't get lost within the site or confused about how to use its various features. The topic of user interface design is a subject in itself, known as Human Computer Interface (HCI) and there are many guidelines and rules on producing easy to use websites. The 'web pages that suck' site includes many examples of bad web page design, as well as articles on good page design: http://www.webpagesthatsuck.com/

A transactional website also needs to run on systems capable of providing a reasonable response time during periods of high demand, since people quickly get bored with a site whose pages load very slowly.

Shopping from home via the Internet is clearly beneficial to some disabled people for whom a trip to high-street shops may be difficult. Most sites however would be difficult for the visually impaired to use. In April 2005 Queen's University in Belfast started a three-year project to help open the Internet to blind people. You can read more about this project at http://news.bbc.co.uk/1/hi/northern_ireland/4457793.stm.

The customer experience

Unless a customer knows exactly what they want, they typically want to browse through items, view detailed specifications (especially with computer and electronic equipment) and compare prices. With a well-designed interface, a website can provide all these facilities to the customer, which is often difficult to achieve in a traditional store. All sites allow customers to search for items. Some sites only provide a simple key word search, more sophisticated sites include multiple criteria searches and searches within restricted categories. Some sites also allow search results to be ordered (most or least expensive first, for example) in a particular way. Many sites provide extensive information on the specification of the products they offer, some offering manufacturers data sheets or links to the manufacturers website for further details. Some sites also allow customers to rate products and make these comments available to prospective purchasers (online book seller Amazon is an example of this). This can help buyers make up their mind and is another example of a feature that is not available with traditional shopping.

As long as their facilities are reasonably easy to use, they can enhance the customer experience and provide another reason to shop online and return to the sites that provide the best experience.

Theory into practice

Investigate the design of another commercial website. In terms of design, ease of use and navigation, what are its strengths and weaknesses?

You could also ask other people, such as members of your family, to rate the different sites based on the facilities they provide.

Assessment activity

Research the various types of e-commerce website and evaluate them in terms of ease of use and the facilities they provide. The questions you should ask include:

* How easy is it to find the products you want?
* Is a range of search options provided?
* Can lists of matching items be displayed in different orders (cheapest first, most popular first, etc.)?
* Was sufficient information provided to enable you to choose between similar products?

Assessment hint

✓ Briefly describe the main features of the site's design.

✓✓✓ Find and investigate suitable sites independently and provide a comprehensive description of the site

> **Signpost for e-portfolio evidence**
>
> Save this work in your portfolio. It could contribute towards covering assessment evidence (a).

2.4 Back-office processes

While the web pages you interact with are the most obvious part of a transactional website, it is the software that runs on the server computers that make the whole shopping process work. The choices you make on the web pages and the information you enter are all transferred back to the website's server computers for processing. This processing includes the following:

* real-time tracking of customers' actions
* the maintenance of the virtual shopping basket
* identification and authentication routines
* payment processing
* stock control
* despatch and delivery.

These software systems are connected to other systems within the company, some of which may predate the web-based system, and also to other systems outside the company, such as the credit card authorisation system. In this section we shall look at each stage of a typical online purchase again, this time concentrating on what happens in the 'back office' where the seller's web server computers are located.

> **Key term**
>
> A *web server* is a computer which runs software that responds to requests to display web pages. A website is accessed using its Internet address (i.e. www.domainname.suffix), which is used to find the appropriate web server computer that holds the page.

FIGURE 2.8 *The search phase*

During the search and select phase, the user makes choices and enters information into the web page he or she is viewing. This data is transferred back to the server and used to query the product database. The resulting data is used to produce a web page that shows the products that match the search criteria. This page is then transmitted back to the user. As well as including product and price information, stock or estimated delivery date information may also be extracted from the product database for inclusion in the data that is sent back to the user. This process is show in diagrammatic form in Figure 2.8.

Real-time tracking of customer's actions

Each time a user visits the transactional website, a record is created in the server's database of the visit, which is commonly known as the session. Each session is identified by an ID number. The session record is used to track and hold information about the user's visit while he or she is using the site.

Maintenance of the virtual shopping basket

Having found the product he or she requires, the user may then place it in the virtual shopping basket. The details of the product

FIGURE 2.9 *The shopping basket*

that has been chosen and the quantity required are recorded as part of the session data. The user may search for and add many different items in the shopping basket, and the session record maintains a list of the items in the basket. In some cases a user may browse the website and add items to the basket but leave the site without purchasing anything. Some sites do allow users to maintain a saved shopping basket or wish list, which they can access next time they visit the site. The diagram in Figure 2.9 shows the main data flows associated with placing an item in the shopping basket.

Identification and authentication routines

When the user has finished shopping and goes to the checkout page on the site, he or she must first log on. If he or she is a new user, he or she enters his or her personal details and this information is transmitted to the server and recorded in the registered user database. If the customer is an existing user, his or her authentication information (username and password) is transmitted to the server and checked against the database to ensure it matches the recorded credentials (see Figure 2.10).

From this stage on, the transactions between user and website are usually done using a secure connection.

> **Key term**
>
> A *secure connection* is used to protect information (such as credit card numbers and personal information) as it is transmitted from the customer to the website he or she is using. The data sent is encrypted so no one else can read it. When you enter a secure connection, a dialogue box appears telling you that you are about use a secure connection, as shown in Figure 2.11. A similar dialogue box also appears when you exit the secure connection, warning you that you are about to do so. While you are using a secure connection a padlock icon appears in the Status bar at the bottom of the browser window.

FIGURE 2.10 *Log on*

Payment processing

Once the user has logged on or registered, the server will calculate the total sales price using the session data about the items in his or her shopping basket and will apply the site rules about postage and packing, etc. The user will then be asked to confirm that he or she wishes to proceed with the purchase. If the user does, the server must then either ask the user for his or her credit card details and obtain authorisation for the sale from the user's credit card company. This involves transmitting the user's credit card details and the amount of the sale to the credit card company's authorisation computer. (Some servers may already have the user's credit card details on their registered

FIGURE 2.11 *Opening a secure connection*

user database with the user's authorisation. In this case, they simply extract the relevant details from the database to transmit to the credit card company.) Once authorisation has been obtained, the server will create a record on the transaction database, recording all the details of the sale. It will also update the stock levels on the product database since the items in the sale are no longer 'in stock': they are awaiting despatch to the customer.

Stock control, despatch and delivery

The server will also send a message to the warehouse computer notifying it that a sale has been made and that the goods need to be despatched. Using the data recorded on the transaction database, the warehouse computer will print off a picking list and an address label so that the warehouse personnel can pick and pack the items purchased and stick the address label on the package ready for it to be collected by the delivery company. The main data flows for this step are shown in Figure 2.12.

Theory into practice

What software do people use to create transactional websites? There are a number of software systems that are currently in use, including Dreamweaver and Cold Fusion from Macromedia and ASP® from Microsoft. Find out what features these and other systems provide and how they can be used to create transactional websites.

Assessment activity

Using an e-commerce website you are familiar with, create detailed diagrams showing the events involved in an online purchase. The diagrams should show the flow of information between the user, the website and other back office processes. The diagrams should show how the virtual shopping is maintained, how customers are identified and authorised, and how payment is processed. They should also show how the system links with stock control, despatch and delivery.

Assessment hint

✓ Produce a diagram which gives an outline of the purchase process.

✓✓✓ Produce diagrams which give a complete and accurate picture of the process and are effectively presented.

Signpost for e-portfolio evidence

This activity covers assessment evidence (b).

2.5 E-customers

As you discovered when investigating transactional websites, an essential part of completing an online transaction is registering the customer and collecting his or her details. This provides an vital information bank that is an important resource for the selling organisation, and one that it is not always possible for traditional (non-Internet) sellers to collect. One of the most important pieces of information is the customer's email address. Once this has been collected, the seller has a way to update the customer regularly on the latest offers and new products. Anyone who has purchased from an Internet site will know that he or she is guaranteed regular emails from the organisation advertising their goods or services.

FIGURE 2.12 *Completing the sale*

Analysis of purchase histories and sales information

In addition to the personal information collected when a customer registers with a site, data is also collected about every sale that is made. This information needs to be collected in order to complete the sale. However, it is also analysed for marketing purposes. Such information can help to identify a number of important things:

* which products are selling the best, and which are increasing and decreasing in their sales
* what category of products sells the best
* how sales vary at different times of the year
* which region of the country sales come from.

This data can be used to:

* plan capacity at the warehouse
* measure the effectiveness of advertising
* plan new products or product ranges
* forward-order stock to meet anticipated demand.

The careful analysis of this kind of data can ensure that the company is run in a efficient way: it can help make sure that there is the right kind and quantity of goods in the warehouse and that the warehouse in not overstocked (no one wants to have a warehouse full of Christmas decorations on the 26 December!) as this costs money.

Think it over...

What website and traditional sellers have you come across that run loyalty schemes? What sort of companies tend to run these schemes? Why do they run them? What benefits are there for the companies that run the schemes?

Loyalty schemes

Many online stores, in common with many traditional sellers, operate loyalty schemes. These provide purchasers with points or e-vouchers that can be collected and exchanged for discounts on goods. These schemes are designed to encourage purchasers to visit the store repeatedly.

Surveys

Surveys or questionnaires are used by some sites to collect information about customers. Sites often ask new users where they heard about the site. This information is used to judge the effectiveness of various types of marketing. However, it is difficult to collect very much information this way as users are often unwilling to spend a lot of time filling them in.

Competitions

Competitions and special offers are used by some sites to encourage users to buy items and to return to the site. Some companies also run traditional competitions on chocolate or drinks wrappers that require the entrant to go to the company's website, thereby encouraging visitors to their site.

Cookies

A cookie is a text file that a web server can store on a user's hard disk when he or she views a page from that server. Cookies store some information about your visit to the web page, and they are generally used so that the web server can identify you. For example, many e-commerce websites use cookies to identify users who have visited the website previously. They are also used by the server to keep track of users and their shopping trolley contents. When you open a shopping web page, a cookie is normally created on your machine with a unique session ID number in it, allocated by the server. Each time you put an item in your shopping trolley, the web server checks and records the ID number from the cookie and so keeps track of which shopping trolley items belong to which user.

Cookies do sometimes get users worried as they don't like the idea of other people saving files on their computer, but it is important to realise that the cookies by themselves are just files (not programs) and therefore they do not represent much of a security risk. There are also some concerns over privacy and cookies. Cookies can be used to record information about which pages within a site you have visited and therefore they build up a profile of the products you might be interested in but have not yet bought. This information could be used to target marketing specifically at you, and your interests.

> **Theory into practice**
>
> Investigate the cookies on your PC at home or in the classroom. What picture do they build up of you? Look at the way cookies track which websites you have visited.

Spyware

Spyware is the name often given to advertising-supported software. This is normally used by shareware authors to make money from a product, other than by users paying for the licence. An example is the 'Gator' program which is included in some freeware and shareware programs. This program helps you fill out online forms (by remembering your details), but it also sends information about your web-surfing habits back to the company that produces the program and pops up adverts on your PC.

> **Key term**
>
> *Shareware* is software that can be obtained and downloaded free of charge. The software, however, is copyright and can only be used for an evaluation period before a payment needs to be made.

Advertising and media companies offer software that displays banner adverts to shareware authors to add to the products they have created. In return, the authors receive a portion of the revenue from the advert sales. This might seem fairly harmless, even if the adverts are annoying, but the problem with these spyware programs is that, as well as displaying the adverts, they also gather statistics of various types (the Internet sites you visit and the products you might be interested in, for example) and transmit these statistics back to the organisation that originally provided the spyware program. Most of the statistics gathered are quite harmless, and spy ware is not illegal. Nonetheless, many people are uncomfortable with the idea of data about them being gathered and transmitted.

All these techniques are used to enable the online seller to gather as much information as possible about their customers. Unlike traditional shops, there is no personal contact between the buyer and seller and the opportunity to build loyalty based on a personal relationship does not exist. This, coupled with the ease with which searches and price comparisons can be made, makes customer loyalty difficult for the online seller to build. Collecting information about a customer's interests and the sort of products they like enables a site to provide customised marketing targeted at individuals and groups of customers. Sites can also attempt to obtain a competitive advantage over their competitors by the following methods:

* *Offering a personalised service*: this can be done, for example, by sending what appear to be personalised emails that offer goods and services that the customer's profile suggests he or she may be interested in.

* *Persuading customers to spend more*: a number of sites provide encouragement to purchase additional items with 'other customers who bought this item also bought the following' sections (Amazon is an example of this), or lists of accessories or additional items which relate to items already selected.

* *Predicting market trends*: by analysing sales trends, sites can see, for example, which items are becoming less popular, and so can offer them at a discount to get rid of stock. They may also be able to spot which products are becoming more popular and so order more to meet the anticipated demand.

* *Reduce wastage*: this is also linked to spotting trends in sales and is particularly important for sites that sell perishable goods, such as supermarkets or sites that sell flowers. If they buy in too little stock they will be unable to meet the demand; if they buy too much, goods will be wasted.

Knowledge check

1 Why do companies collect information about the individuals who visit their website?
2 What methods are used to attract and retain customers?

2.6 E-consumer awareness

While collecting information about customers and their purchases is useful for the seller, e-customers need to be aware of what information is held, how accurate it is, who has access to that information and how it is used. They need to be sure that the information collected is being protected against theft and misuse. They need to know how accurate the information being held about them is. They also need to be aware of some of the more intrusive methods that can be used to collect information and how to protect themselves against methods that may be used by some unscrupulous sites.

People are naturally worried about handing over personal and financial information, especially with the recent increase in identity fraud, where criminals steal individual's identity (personal details, account numbers, etc.) and then use this data to obtain money from their bank accounts or on their behalf (by taking out loans, etc. using the stolen identity). Transactional websites need to make sure customers are confident to hand over such information, and assure them that it will be used properly and stored securely.

Data Protection Act

Customers purchasing from UK-based sites are, of course, protected by the Data Protection Act (DPA). This requires companies that hold personal information about living individuals to keep that information:

* secure from unauthorised access
* accurate and up to date

> **Theory into practice**
>
> Find out more about the DPA and what companies must do and what they must not do. A good place to start is the website of the Information Commissioner, which is the government body that looks after data protection issues, see www.informationcommissioner.gov.uk (a link to their site is available at www.heinemann.co.uk/hotlinks (express code 2008P)).

* for no longer than is necessary
* only for the purpose it was gathered.

Companies that keep personal information must register with the Data Protection Registrar and, if they break the rules, they face legal action.

Customers are also protected by the Distance Selling Regulations which apply to goods purchased by phone (mail order), over the Internet or via TV. The protection provided includes:

* the customer has the right to receive clear, accurate information about the goods
* goods must be delivered within 30 days unless agreed otherwise
* the customer has a 'cooling-off period' that allows him or her to withdraw from the sale for up to seven days after the sale is made (this does not apply to some goods, such as perishable items and unsealed CDs and DVDs)
* the company must refund the customer if his or her credit card is used fraudulently.

The online buyer is also protected by the same regulations that cover goods sold by traditional methods, such as:

* the Sale of Goods Act, which requires that goods are of satisfactory quality and gives the customer the right to obtain a replacement if a fault is discovered

> **CASE STUDY**
>
> *'Phishing'*
>
> Online banking has naturally been a target for criminal activity. So called 'phishing' (a misspelling of the word 'fishing') involves an attempt to get an unsuspecting customer of the online bank to reveal his or her personal details, such as username, password and security codes. This is done by sending an email to the customer which purports to be from the person's bank, and which asks the person to follow a hyperlink that takes him or her to a page which is made to look like one of the genuine bank's pages. Once at this bogus page, the customer fills in his or her account details and these are collected by the criminals, who can use this information to transfer the money into the criminals' account. Up to November 2004, around 2,000 people had been victims of these scams, with £4.5 million lost (although the banks have refunded the money to the customers).
>
> **How can banks protect their customers from these types of attacks? You may find it helpful to visit the anti-fraud website set up by the banks at www.banksafeonline.org.uk (a link to their site is available at www.heinemann.co.uk/hotlinks (express code 2008P)).**

* the regulations of the Advertising Standards Authority, which require that adverts are legal, decent, honest and truthful.

> **Theory into practice**
>
> Find more about the distance-selling regulations at the DTI (Department of Trade and Industry) website (*www.dti.gov.uk/ccp/topics1/ecomm.htm;* a link to their site is available at *www.heinemann.co.uk/hotlinks* (express code 2008P)).

2.7 Security

As we have already mentioned, security is a big issue with online buying. People are naturally cautious where money is involved, and the thought of personal details, particularly credit or debit card information, being hijacked by cyber criminals puts some people off shopping on the Internet. Organisations that want to operate successfully online must take the threats to data security seriously in order to win their customers' confidence and trust.

Organisations can try to protect themselves against these kinds of attacks by using:

* risk assessments
* physical security
* user IDs and access right
* encryption
* secure electronic transactions
* firewalls
* virus protection.

Each of these techniques is described below.

Risk assessment

Before any organisation can arrange with its bank to accept payments electronically over the Internet, it must carry out a risk assessment which estimates how exposed the organisation is to the risk that the customer will not pay for the goods. There are two main reasons why a customer may not pay for the goods:

* the customer may request a refund from the credit card company (for example, if the goods are faulty or are never delivered – known as a charge-back)
* the customer's card has been stolen.

> **Key term**
>
> *Exposure to risk* is an estimate of how likely an event will take place. The estimation is based on a number of factors. Insurance companies, for example, estimate how exposed to risk a person or organisation is when they calculate premiums.

Risk assessment for an online business is based on a number of factors:

* *The amount of goods the company estimates it will sell*: the more goods that are sold, the greater the likelihood of problems
* *The average transaction size*: higher-value items are more likely to cause problems
* *Time taken from payment to order delivery*: the longer it takes the company to deliver the goods, the greater the risk that the customer will cancel his or her payment
* *Length of time in business*: a start-up company represents a greater risk than an established one
* *Business classification*: different business sectors have different risks. For example, if you purchase an airline ticket online, you have to turn up at the airport to take the flight. However, if you purchase a CD online you can always claim it was never delivered, or copy and return it and claim a refund
* *The security the organisation puts in place*: the more secure the bank thinks an organisation's website and overall system is, the less the risk.

Having estimated the risk, the bank will require the organisation to pay a bond (like an insurance premium) to cover the risk. You can find more information about electronic payments and risk assessment at the Electronic Payment website (www.electronic-payments.co.uk; a link to their site is available at www.heinemann.co.uk/hotlinks (express code 2008P)).

Physical security

The data held on the selling organisation's web servers and other computers must be physically secure as well as secure from attack via electronic means. This means the computers must be locked in a room to which only authorised staff have the key. Copies of backup disks or tapes must also be kept secure. It is unwise to store backups in the same room as the server (since a fire or other catastrophe could destroy both), so they should be stored securely at another site.

User IDs and access rights

Networked multi-user computer systems have usernames to identify individual users. Local users of the web servers of an Internet shopping site would include technicians, managers, customer service staff and warehouse personnel. Each of these users must have his or her own username and password. Different users will need to gain access to different parts of the system and the data held on it. Personal data about the site's customers, for example, must be protected against unauthorised access because:

* it is a requirement of the Data Protection Act that personal information cannot be viewed by people who do not need to see the information
* this information is commercially sensitive. The organisation would not want a competitor to able to get hold of a list of customers' email addresses, for example
* details of people's credit cards must be protected from unauthorised access.

In order to protect data held on the system, the administrator must set the access rights to sensitive data files so that only those users who are authorised to see them can do so.

Encryption

This is a technique for encoding sensitive information (such as credit card details) when it is sent over the Internet so that only the site that the data is intended for can decode it. Most e-commerce websites use a type of encryption known as secure sockets layer (SSL) encryption when this type of data is being sent.

Secure electronic transactions (SET)

SET is a networking protocol developed by the credit card organisations Visa and MasterCard. It is designed to ensure the security of electronic credit

CASE STUDY

The Sasser Internet worm

In May 2004 the Sasser Internet worm virus caused chaos. It hit hundreds of thousands of computers across the world, causing them continuously to shut down and then reboot. The virus was created by an 18-year-old German student. Unlike other viruses, Sasser did not require the computer users to download a file or open an email – it invaded the machines directly via the Internet exploiting a loop-hole in recent versions of Microsoft operating systems including Windows 2000 and XP. Only those computers which had the very latest Microsoft updates could prevent the virus infecting them. The required update was only released a couple of weeks before the virus started infecting machines.

card transactions made over the Internet. SET encrypts messages sent between the buyer and the seller so they cannot easily be read by anyone else.

Firewalls

To protect their web servers and other computers from outside electronic attack, Internet shops commonly use a firewall. This is device that provides a gateway between the company's internal network and the external Internet. The software in a firewall inspects incoming data and only allows data through into the internal network if it is legitimate. This helps to prevent hackers from trying to gain information about the systems and data within the organisation.

Virus protection

Viruses are a major problem on the Internet. Viruses can damage data held on computers and can also use infected computers for unauthorised purposes, such as sending emails and replicating themselves. It is vital, therefore, that organisations running e-commerce website protect their machines from virus attack by installing virus-detecting software and updating it regularly so that it can catch the latest viruses.

Assessment activity

Investigate three ways in which the customer data that is collected by organisations via their website could be misused. You will need to describe these threats and evaluate their likely impact. You will also need to describe and evaluate the protective measures that organisations can take to defend themselves against each of these threats. In addition, describe and evaluate two examples of legislation which is relevant to this area.

Assessment hint

- ✓ Describe some of the potential threats and the measures taken to protect customer data.
- ✓✓ Include some assessment of the effectiveness of the protective measures taken

Signpost for e-portfolio evidence

This activity covers assessment evidence (c).

2.8 The database

As you discovered when we looked at the back office processes that take place on the web server of a transactional website, databases have a very important role to play. They store key information which makes the site work:

* details of the products on offer (prices and specifications, etc.)
* stock levels of the products
* registered customers' details
* details of orders placed.

Each of these sets of information is stored in a table so that the complete database contains many different tables.

Through out this section we shall be using an example database to demonstrate how the database can be set up and analysed. The database is designed to support an imaginary online DVD store called AJ's DVDs.

Selecting appropriate field types and formats

Before you use a database you must decide how the data to be stored in the database will be structured (i.e. how the data is divided up into tables and fields). A table is a collection of data about a particular subject, such as customers or products; fields are individual items of data within the table. The decisions you make about the database structure will depend upon the nature of the data (i.e. where it comes from and what it describes) and what information you will want to extract from the database.

A single table consists of many records, and each record is split into different fields which store a particular piece of data. So, for example, the DVD list table would have fields for the DVD number, Title, Category, Rating, Price and so on (see Figure 2.13).

DVD_number	Title	Category	Rating	Price
1	The Italian Job	Thriller	U	£8.99
2	The Matrix	Thriller	18	£12.99
3	The Lion King	Childrens	U	£10.99
4	Die Another Day	Thriller	12	£1.99
5	8 Mile	Drama	18	£15.99
6	Lord of the Rings	Drama	12	£12.50
7	Jonny English	Comedy	U	£2.50
8	4 Wedding and a funeral	Comedy	18	£10.25
9	Diamonds are forever	Thriller	12	£8.25
10	The jungle book	Childrens	U	£7.50
11	Who framed Roger Rabbit	Childrens	U	£9.99
12	Toy Story	Childrens	U	£10.50
13	Star Wars - The empire s	Thriller	12	£13.45
14	My big fat Greek wedding	Comedy	U	£9.99
15	Flubber	Comedy	U	£10.50
16	The fast and the furious	Thriller	18	£12.50

FIGURE 2.13 *Tables, records and fields*

When creating a database table, you will need to decide what fields are needed in the table and what format the data in the fields will be in. There are two basic data types, numbers and text, but there are many variations of the basic types. For example, numbers can be whole numbers, numbers with a certain number of digits after the decimal point or numbers formatted in a particular way, such as currency. A date is another type of numeric data type, and with this type different formats can be set (for example, a short date format such as 26/10/04 or a longer format such as 26th October 2004).

Theory into practice

The database for AJ's DVD store contains information about the customers who are registered with the site in the Customer table, and details of the DVDs which are offered for sales in a table called DVD list. The fields within the Customer table and the data types for those fields are shown in Figure 2.14.

Customer : Table

Field Name	Data Type
Customer Number	AutoNumber
Title	Text
First name	Text
Family name	Text
Age	Number
e-mail address	Text
Address	Text
Town	Text
Postcode	Text

FIGURE 2.14 *Fields in the Customer table*

Most database tables have a special field which is used as a unique identifier for each record. This is called the primary key, and it is usual to choose a made-up value, such as an ID or account number, rather than some real data such as a person's name, to ensure the value is unique.

Creating simple validation rules

It is important that the data contained in a database is accurate and valid. Creating validation rules can help ensure the data entered into the database is valid. Some validation is done automatically by the database software. For example, if you create a field with a date data type, the software will not allow you to enter an invalid date, such as 26/13/04. However, you can add further validation to ensure data is reasonable. For example, if you have a field in the Customer table for the customer's date for birth, today's date, although a valid date, could not be a correct entry. In fact, since all online shops require payment to be made by credit or debit cards and these are only available to people aged

> **Theory into practice**
>
> The Customer table in AJ's DVD store database contains a field called Age, which is used to store the customers' ages. The store does not accept orders from anyone under 18 and a value higher than 120 would of course be invalid! Therefore a validation rule can be applied which says that Age must be equal to or greater than 18 and less than 120. Figure 2.15 shows how this validation rule can be applied using Microsoft Access. The validation text is the message that appears on the screen if an age outside these boundaries is entered.
>
> What other validation could you add for the fields in the Customer and DVD list tables?

FIGURE 2.15 *Validation for the Age field*

18 or over, you could create a validation rule for the date of birth field that says the person must be 18 or over.

Creating a one-to-many relationship between tables

Database systems allow relationships to be set up between different tables so that, for example, records on the Order table can be related to the customers who placed the order, and whose details are stored on the Customer table. This type of relationship is sometimes called a one-to-many relationship, because one customer on the Customer table may have many related orders on the Order table.

> **Key term**
>
> A *one-to-many relationship* can exist between records on two different tables. The table which is at the 'one' end of the relationship has individual records which can be related to many records on the other table. So, for example, in a doctors' surgery database each doctor on the Doctor table can be related to many patients on a Patient table.

Relationships like these are created by using a field from the 'one' side of the relationship, usually the primary key field, and placing the value in that key field into a field on the 'many' side of the relationship. Therefore when you look at records on the Order table, you know which customer placed the order because Customer number is one of the fields in the order record. (See Figure 2.16 for a diagrammatic representation of this relationship.)

In a similar way, all the details of the DVD that has been ordered do not need to be recorded on the Order table, only the DVD number is required. This is also a one-to-many relationship since one DVD will appear on many orders.

Customer Table

Customer ID	Title	First name	Family Name
001	Mr	John	Smith
002	Ms	Alice	Johes
003	Mr	Ali	Hassan

Orders Table

Purchase No.	Customer ID	Date
1	003	10/4/05
2	002	11/5/05
3	002	11/5/05

FIGURE 2.16 *The relationship between customers and orders*

Using a single table to record an order has a serious restriction. What if a customer wanted to order more than one DVD? To deal with this possibility, you need to split the Order table into two tables. One, which we shall call the Order header, will store the information about the order that does not change no matter how many DVDs are on the order, such as the order number, the customer number and the date of the order. The other table we shall call the Order items: this has one record for each DVD ordered. It is related to the Order header table using the order number and it also has fields for the DVD number and the quantity. The DVD number is used to link records on this table to the DVD list table, where the full details of the DVD, such as the title, price and rating, are held. The relationships that exist between these four tables are shown in Figure 2.17.

Importing a given data set

In order to investigate how databases can be used to analyse data and to identify trends such as buying habits, you need to deal with databases that have a large number of records.

FIGURE 2.17 *Relationships between tables*

Rather than having to key in hundreds of records it is much simpler to import a ready-prepared set of data. Data sets are normally prepared in a text file, so they can be imported into a variety of different database programs.

> **Key term**
>
> A *comma separated values (CSV)* file is a text file which can be used to store database records. Each field on the file is separated by a comma, and each record is separated by a carriage return. CSV files are sometimes used to transfer data between systems since they can be easily exported and imported.

The most common way of formatting data in a text file is to use a comma to separate each field and a carriage return to separate each record. These type of files are sometimes called CSV files, which stands for comma separated values.

As these are text files you can view them in a text editor such as Microsoft Notepad (Figure 2.18 shows a CSV file displayed in Notepad). The data in it could be used to populate the DVD list table on AJ's DVDs database.

In some CSV files, the first line contains the field names, but in this example it does not. This is not a problem as you can assign field names when the

FIGURE 2.18 *A CSV file*

UNIT 2: THE DIGITAL ECONOMY

data is imported. However you will need to decide or find out what each field represents so that you can choose appropriate field names and data types.

To import a CSV file into Microsoft Access, you need to have an existing database open, even if it does not yet contain any tables. Then from the **File** menu, select: **Get external data**, and, from the sub-menu: **Import**. You will then see the Open File dialogue box where you need to select the CSV file you want to import. Make sure you choose **Text Files** from the **Files of type** drop-down box at the bottom of the dialogue box. The Import Text Wizard will then start, showing the first few lines of the file you have selected, as shown in Figure 2.19.

You should not need to make any changes to the standard setting, so just click: **Next** to move to the next step. This will show the data split up into fields. If your data has field names as its first row, make sure that option is selected (see Figure 2.20).

The next step allows you to choose whether the data should be appended to an existing table in the database or placed in a new table. You will probably want to add the data to a new table. Click: **Next** to go to the next step, which is where you will add field names and data types to the data. For each field you will need to enter a field name and check the data type has been correctly set (see Figure 2.21). The first field in this example can be named **Reference Number.**

This field should also be indexed as the primary (unique) key for the table. You now click on the next column of the data and name this field, and so on until all the fields are named (see Figure 2.22).

FIGURE 2.19 Import Text Wizard, step 1

FIGURE 2.21 Naming the first field

FIGURE 2.20 Import Text Wizard, step 2

FIGURE 2.22 Naming the fields

GCE AS Level Applied ICT

The next step of the wizard will ask you for a primary key, so you can choose the name of the first field (Reference number) we named from the drop-down box.

The final step of the wizard will ask you to name the table itself. You will need to check that all the data has been imported correctly by comparing the contents of the original text CSV file with the table that has been created.

Using queries to sort and extract valid and meaningful information

Queries answer questions about your data. They are able to combine data from different related tables and to select records which match certain criteria. Queries can also select the fields you wish to view and sort the data in whatever order you choose. Because of their powerful ability to manipulate data in these ways, queries are the key tools for analysing data. We shall investigate how queries can be used with a number of examples.

Selecting fields and sorting data

The ability to sort data by any field and by multiple fields is a useful tool. You could, for example, sort the records on the DVD list table in order of the number of sales made. This would tell you which DVDs were most popular. You could also sort the records first by the category the DVD is in, then by sales made. This would show what the most popular DVD in each category was.

Theory into practice

In order to create a query in Microsoft Access you first have to choose the *Queries* option from the database control centre, then select: *Create query in Design view* from the panel on the right, as shown in Figure 2.23.

This will display the Query grid, with the Select Table dialogue in front of it. Choose the DVD list table from the Select Table dialogue box, click: *Add* to add the table to the Query grid, then click: *Close* to close the Select Table dialogue box. Your screen should now look like Figure 2.24.

In this example we shall only display the fields Title, Category and Sales_made. Select each of those fields in turn and drag them from the table into the top row of the Query grid, each in their own column (see Figure 2.25).

Finally, we want to sort the records by the Sales_made field, so click in the row labelled *Sort*, in the Sales_made column, and select: *Descending* from the drop-down list (see Figure 2.26).

The query can now be run by going to the *Query* menu and choosing the *Run* option. This will show the list of DVDs with the DVD with the highest number of sales first (Figure 2.27).

FIGURE 2.23 *Creating a query*

FIGURE 2.24 *The Query grid*

FIGURE 2.25 Selecting the required fields

FIGURE 2.26 Sorting the records

FIGURE 2.27 The DVD with the highest number of sales

You can also sort records by multiple fields. If you click in the **Sort** box below the Category field and choose **Ascending** and run the query again, you will see the DVDs listed alphabetically (since Category is a text field it is sorted alphabetically), and then within each category the films are listed with the highest-selling one first. Because the Category field is shown before (to the left of) the Sales_made field in the Query grid, the data is sorted by that field first. If you have these fields the other way around you will not get meaningful results. You can, of course, save a query so that you can run it anytime you wish by going to the **File** menu, choosing: **Save** and giving the query a suitable name.

Combining data from different tables

With a query you can display fields from different, related tables.

Theory into practice

For example, suppose you wanted to see how many orders each customer had placed. To create a query to show this information, you would return to the Query section of the database control centre and double-click the *Create a new query in Design view* option as before, click on: *Customer* in the Select Table dialogue box, then click: *Add*, then on the *Order header* table and also *Add*, then *Close*. The two tables will now be shown with the relationship between them also visible, as shown in Figure 2.28.

FIGURE 2.28 *Related tables in the Query grid*

Now drag the First name and Family name fields from the Customer table and the Date field from the Order header field into the Query grid. Set the *Sort* box for the Family name field to *Ascending* so that the customers will be displayed in alphabetical order, then run the query. Don't forget to save this query, calling it *Customers and Orders* as we will use it later to create a report.

Filtering records using selection criteria

One of the most powerful data analysis tools is the ability to select certain records from your data based on the criteria you set.

Theory into practice

Each of the DVDs on the database is categorised into children's, drama, comedy, etc. Suppose you wanted to list only those DVDs in a certain category – comedy, for example. To do this you would create a new query as before and add the DVD list table to the query. Then drag the Title and the Category fields into the Query grid and under the Category column. In the row labelled *Criteria* you would key in *Comedy*, as shown in Figure 2.29.

FIGURE 2.29 *Entering a simple query criterion*

Now run the query and only those DVDs in the comedy category will be displayed

Let's look at a slightly more complex example of how to use criteria within a query. How could you list all the orders placed in a certain month, say, for example, November 2004?

Theory into practice

Follow the instructions given previously to bring both the Order header and the Customer tables into the query, and drag the Order number, Customer number and Date fields from the Order header table into the Query grid and the First name and Family name fields from the Customer table. In the Query grid under the Date column and in the row labelled *Criteria* key in *Between 1/11/2004 And 30/11/2004*, as shown in Figure 2.30.

FIGURE 2.30 *Entering a more complex query criterion*

Now run the query and only those order placed in November 2004 will be displayed.

Producing reports to present information clearly

Database reports enable you to format the information that has been extracted from the database using a query and to present it clearly, professionally and neatly.

To show how a report can be created we will use the Customers and Orders query created earlier. Before starting work on the report we will make the query a little more sophisticated so that it shows not only when each customer placed an order, but also what he or she actually ordered.

Theory into practice

Open the query in Design view and then go to the *View* menu. Choose: *Show table* and then add the Order items and DVD list tables. Drag the DVD title from the DVD list table and the Quantity from the Order items table into the Query grid. Also drag the Order number field from the Order header table to the first column of the Query grid and set this field to be sorted *Ascending* (that way all the orders will be shown together in order). Your query should now look like that show in Figure 2.31.

FIGURE 2.31 *The modified Customers and Orders query*

If you now run the query, you will see a list of all the orders along with details of which DVDs were ordered. However, the data is not displayed in an organised way since the customer's name is repeated for each DVD he or she ordered. With a report the data can be formatted so that the customer name and the date of the order are displayed first, then the DVDs ordered shown underneath.

Theory into practice

Save this modified version of the query then return to the database control centre and choose the *Reports* option and double-click the *Create report by using wizard* option (see Figure 2.32.

FIGURE 2.32 *Creating a report using the wizard*

FIGURE 2.33 *Selecting the fields*

You will then see the first step in the wizard process. Choose the *Customers and Orders* query from the drop-down box, then use the double arrow button to add all the available fields to the list of selected fields (you can, if you wish, only display some of the fields from the query in your report, but in this example we need them all) (see Figure 2.33).

Then click: *Next* to go to the next step in creating the report. This step allows you to choose by which field you would like the data grouped. We want the data grouped by Order header so that all the details of the order (date, customer, etc.) are displayed first and then the items on the order are listed underneath each order (see Figure 2.34).

Click: *Next* and the wizard will ask if you want any groups within the Order header group, but you don't need any in this example, so just click: *Next*. This step asks what sorting and summary options you require for the report. The query is already sorted by Order number, so there is no need to choose any sorting here. The *Summary* button allows any numeric fields to be totalled up (sum) or the

FIGURE 2.34 *Choosing how to group the data in the report*

average, minimum or maximum values displayed. It is quite useful to know how many DVDs were ordered on each order and in total, so select: *Sum* for the Quantity field (see Figure 2.35).

Click: *Next* to go to the next step, where you can choose the layout options for the report. You can leave this set on the default *stepped* layout, and the same is true for the next step where you can choose the style of the report.

(Continued)

Unit 2: The digital economy

Finally, you will be asked what title you want for the report. Something like *Orders Report* would be suitable. The wizard has now been completed and, when you click: *Finish*, the report it has created is displayed in Print Preview, as shown in Figure 2.36.

FIGURE 2.35 Summing the Quantity field

FIGURE 2.36 Completed report

Identifying trends in data

Data collected in the databases of transactional websites contains important information about the buying habits of individual customers and the overall trends that the business is experiencing. Trends are changes that occur over time. For example, in an organisation that sells several types of products, the number of sales made of one type of product may be rising while sales of the other type of product may be falling. It is important that the management of the company is aware of these trends and carries out marketing activities or makes other changes in the business to take advantage of positive trends and to avoid the consequences of negatives ones. To identify and analyse trends within data, you will need to produce summary reports which show how values, such as the number or value of sales made, have changed over time.

Theory into practice

Suppose we wanted to look at the total value of the sales made each month by AJ's DVDs. The first step it to create a query which brings together the required data. To do this you create a new query in Design view as before, bringing in the Order header, Order items and DVD list tables. From the Order header table you include the Date field in the query, from the Order items you include the DVD number and Quantity and from the DVD list table the Price is included. This query also needs some data added that is derived from these fields. You want to look at the sales made each month over a whole year so you need to include a field which shows the month the sale was made. This can be derived from the Date field. To do this, go to the next blank column in the Query grid and key in the field row:

(Continued)

Month: DatePart("m",[Date])

This creates a new field in the query called *Month*. It uses the DatePart function to extract the month (as indicated by the "m") from the field called Date (as indicated by [Date]).

In order to restrict the data to a particular year, a criterion needs to be added to the Date field column. So to see orders in 2003 you would enter *Between 01/01/2003 And 31/12/2003.* This field should also be sorted to ensure the orders are shown in date order. The Query grid should now look like Figure 2.37.

FIGURE 2.37 *Adding a Month field to the query*

The other field you need to add is the total price of each order item. The price of the individual DVD is already in the query, but this needs to be multiplied by the quantity in order to give the total price. To do this the following statement is added to the next column in the Query grid, in the Field row:

Total price: [Quantity]*[Price]

This adds another field to the query, called Total price. If the query is now run, this new field will be displayed.

The query in now complete, but is in not very easy to identify any trends from its output because it does not total up the orders each month. To do this you need to create a report. The Report Wizard can be used as before, but the data must be grouped by Month, as shown in Figure 2.38.

FIGURE 2.38 *Grouping the report by Month*

Summary Options is used to sum up the total prices for each order item for each month, as shown in Figure 2.39.

The other options in the Report Wizard can be left at their default values, and the resulting report will list the sales made each month, with the number and value of sales made shown at the end of each month's list, as shown in Figure 2.40.

FIGURE 2.39 *Summary Options*

Looking at the completed report will enable you to identify whether sales have risen or fallen over the year, and which months are the most successful. By modifying the query you could run other reports showing the data from different

(Continued)

years and comparing the monthly sales totals between years.

1. What recommendation might you make to AJ's DVDs based on the analysis of the data that has been done?
2. What other fields could you analyse to attempt to identify relevant sales trends in this data?

FIGURE 2.40 *The completed report*

Databases are at the heart of transactional websites. The day-to-day running of sites relies on them as they the provide product, stock and user information which drives the website. They are also used to record and process each sale. Databases also provide a goldmine of marketing information which management can analyse and use to target and direct their sales and marketing strategy.

2.9 ICT skills

There are a number of ICT skills you will need to complete this unit:

* production of information flow diagrams
* production of reports
* internet research skills
* use of database software to store and manipulate data.

Internet research skills are covered in Unit 1 and use of database software in section 2.8 of Unit 2; this section discusses production of information flow diagrams and reports.

Producing information flow diagrams

There are many different software applications which provide graphics and diagram drawing facilities, however to add simple diagrams to word processed reports the drawing tools provided in Microsoft Word are perfectly adequate.

Before you can use the drawing tools you must ensure the drawing tool bar is displayed (normally shown at the bottom of the editing window) by clicking the Drawing button in the standard tool bar (see Figure 2.41).

To draw a simple text box, just click on the text box button, then drag out a box where you want it to appear on the page. You can type in the box and apply all the text formatting options you can use with normal text. You can move the box around the page by dragging on the shaded outline, or resize the box by dragging on the handles. If you double click on the shaded outline the **Format text box** dialog will appear where you can modify settings like the colour and thickness of the line around the box and the fill colour of the box.

FIGURE 2.41 *The Word drawing toolbar*

When drawing flow diagrams you may want to include other shaped boxes, for example a decision box is always a diamond shape. All the standard flow chart box shapes can be found in the **AutoShapes** menu, under the flowcharts sub-menu. You can draw these shapes in the same way as the text box. To add text inside them, right click on the shape and choose the **Add text** option. You can format these shapes in the same way as text boxes.

To draw arrows joining up your boxes click on the **Arrow** button in the drawing toolbar and drag out the arrow to where it is required. By default the arrow head goes at the end of the line you draw. You can change this, and the thickness, colour and other format setting by double clicking on the arrow to display the Format shape dialog.

Producing reports

You probably already have the skills to use word processing software, but you need to make sure you use them to produce reports that are professional in appearance. Make sure you:

✶ *Structure the report properly*: your report needs to be divided into sections, including an introduction at the beginning and a summary or conclusions at the end. Sections should have headings and subheadings which are formatted in a consistent and appropriate way.

✶ *Check your report for accuracy*: this involves more than just spell-checking your document. You need to proof read it for errors that the spell-checker will not spot and check that the text makes sense and explains the topics required in your course work.

✱ *Include information from other types of software*: you will need to include screen shots of the web sites you have been investigating in your report. This can be done simply by displaying the required page and pressing the 'print screen' key on the keyboard. The screen image can then be pasted into your report. You can scale and crop the screen print using the image editing tools which can be found on the **Picture** toolbar (if it is not shown when you select the image, go to **View** menu, choose **Toolbars**, then **Picture**). Make sure your screen prints are given a title and are annotated if necessary. You can also include information from a database such as Microsoft Access using screen prints, or you can copy and paste sets of database records into your report.

UNIT ASSESSMENT

For this assessment task, you will need to download one of the example datasets from the Edexcel website. You will need to import this file, which is in CSV format, into a database program such as Microsoft Access as described in the text. Having imported it you will need to check that the record structure is correct (using appropriate data types and validation, for example) then carry out the following tasks:

1. Design three queries which, by sorting and/or selecting certain data, will help you to analyse trends within the data.
2. Create reports to format the data from your queries in a clear and professional way.

Once you have completed these tasks, write a report identifying significant trends within the data (for example, changes in sales patterns) and making recommendations for future action.

Assessment hint

- ✓ Create a simple database structure, carry out some limited testing on the database and extract some valid and meaningful data.
- ✓✓ Create a customised database structure. Test the database to ensure all the functions work correctly, extract valid and meaningful data, and identify some significant trends
- ✓✓✓ Include data validation in the database. Identify significant trends in the data, interpret the output and make recommendations.

Signpost for e-portfolio evidence

Save this work in your e-portfolio. It could contribute towards covering evidence (d) and (e).

UNIT 3

The knowledge worker

Introduction

This unit examines the role of the knowledge worker and his or her ability to make informed decisions using modelling tools and techniques. This unit has a user focus and will explore a range of different spreadsheet models.

> **Key terms**
>
> The term '*knowledge worker*' applies to anyone whose job involves the development or use of knowledge. The term was first used by Peter Drucker in his 1959 book, *Landmarks of Tomorrow*, and it includes anyone in ICT fields, such as designers, programmers, systems analysts, technical writers, academic professionals, researchers, etc.
>
> *Modelling tools and techniques* can be used in a range of applications software. For example, in spreadsheet software there are a number of built-in modelling tools and techniques that can be used to enhance and manipulate worksheets. Modelling tools, for example, can help you to perform advanced calculations, add rules to given sets of data, forecast and predict values for a given point in time.

In this information age, ICT provides us with vast quantities of information and, as ICT users and knowledge workers, we have to make judgements about the sources and accuracy of any information we acquire and must be able to select and manipulate this information so that we can make the correct decisions.

This unit will give you a better understanding of how spreadsheets can be used as a modelling tool to facilitate the decision-making process. In addition, it also explains how problems can be addressed, informed decisions made and which factors impact on the choices we make.

What you need to learn

In completing this unit, you should achieve these learning outcomes:

* Know about the different stages involved in the decision-making process
* Understand the underlying logic and assumptions of decision-making models
* Evaluate decisions made by others in the light of available information
* Assess and evaluate the quality of information given by others
* Make decisions based on information provided by others.

Resource toolkit

To complete this unit, you need these essential resources:

* access to computer hardware including a printer
* access to computer software, in particular Microsoft Word, Excel and PowerPoint and graphics software
* sufficient storage space.

How you will be assessed

This unit is externally assessed through an examination. Further information on the conduct of the examination will be published on the Edexcel website in advance of the examination. In the examination:

* You will work with information provided in a number of e-resources, including a spreadsheet model
* You will use the information provided to add to your knowledge of the scenario and inform you decision-making
* You will be expected to use standard office software effectively (such as spreadsheet software) to help you make, present and justify your decision
* Marks will be awarded for evidence of adherence to relevant standard ways of working.

In preparation for assessment you will be encouraged to:

* work safely and adhere to relevant legislation and codes of practice when carrying out the externally-set practical computer-based activities required for this unit
* investigate the underlying logic/assumptions of models
* learn how to question quality of information they have available
* think critically when analysing problems
* practise using models to help make decisions.

How high can you aim

We have already identified a knowledge worker as 'anyone whose job involves the development or use of knowledge'. Throughout this unit you will be preparing yourself for the external assessment. To support you in this preparation, there are a number of activities and practical tasks such as **Theory into practice**, **Think it over** and **Knowledge checks** that will help you to focus on your external assessment requirements. You will be given more up-to-date examination tips and guidance by your teacher.

To start you in the right direction a **Theory into practice** task has been provided that should enable you to develop your understanding of knowledge workers, what they do and how they use information and ICT in their job roles.

This task will enable you to identify the role of a knowledge worker and help you to understand and appreciate your own role as a knowledge worker.

* Keep a journal or a scrapbook about knowledge workers. The types of evidence you could collect include:
  - information about knowledge workers (possibly job descriptions from adverts or vacancy sheets)
  - articles that you may find on the Internet or in newspapers.
* In one section of your journal/scrapbook, design a table and list the range of different knowledge workers, for example designers, programmers, analysts, and the types of ICT that they may use in their job role.

Ready to start?

Why not keep a log of the time you take to complete this unit. Devise a blank form that you could use to record the time that you spend on this course.

3.1 Problem-solving

We all encounter problems on a daily basis, and some of these are routine, such as the decisions we make in terms of what we wear, how we travel to college, what we eat, etc. Some, however, are more complex, and these more complex problems require more thought as to how they can be addressed. Some sort of decision-making process, therefore, needs to be applied.

If we liken a problem to a system, certain inputs will be needed to initiate the thought process, thus leading to a decision being made. The decision we make will be based on any information we have collected and any prior knowledge we have of the problem. This process can become more complicated, however, because we may suffer from 'information overload' – we have too much information and do not know what to do with it all. For the problem-solving process to work, therefore, we must be able to distinguish between information that is relevant to the problem and information that is not. Anything that is not relevant must be discarded. Finally, we must also be aware that ICT simply provides information – it does not supply knowledge. To acquire knowledge, we must read and assess information so that we understand it and can apply that understanding to other areas of our lives.

To help us understand information and thus acquire knowledge, we can use what is known as a 'systems model'. We add inputs to this system, process these inputs and, from the output we obtain, come to a conclusion, as shown in Figure 3.1.

[Inputs: Initiate thought process] → [Processing: Decision making] → [Outputs: Solution to the problem]

FIGURE 3.1 *A basic systems model for problem-solving*

> **Key term**
>
> Every system has a framework or a *systems model*. This model defines the start of the system (its evolution), the mechanics of the system (how it works, etc.) and the completion of the system (what happens next).

> **Theory into practice**
>
> Apply the systems model of problem-solving to the following two tasks:
>
> 1. Booking a holiday.
> 2. Completing an assignment.
>
> Use Table 3.2 to help you decide:
>
> * the resources required
> * the problems that may be encountered
> * the decisions that need to be taken to overcome these problems.

The processing activities that occur within this systems model will differ depending upon the type of system being used (for example, you might sit down with a pen and a piece of paper to solve a problem – a pen-and-paper system – or you might feed data into a computer – a computerised system). The decision-making process can also be simple or complex (see Table 3.1).

TYPE OF PROBLEM	TYPE OF DECISION-MAKING PROCESS
Simple Doing an assignment	Simple Reading through tasks Carrying out research Produce a draft copy Submit final copy
Complex Finding information about a customer on a database	Complex Accessing a central resource such as a database Searching information Sorting and selecting specific details

TABLE 3.1 *Examples of simple and complex decisions*

TASK	RESOURCES	PROBLEMS ENCOUNTERED	DECISIONS
Booking a holiday			
Completing an assignment			

TABLE 3.2 *Problem-solving and decision-making*

3.2 The decision-making process

When you are making decisions, you need to ensure that you are in possession of all the facts to enable you to make the right decision. The decision-making process should, therefore, be based on all the information you already have or can acquire.

You make decisions every second of every day, at home, at work, at college or socially. At work or college, the decisions you make vary from being quite simple (for example, what time shall I have a coffee break?) to quite complex (for example, how should I market this new product?). For knowledge workers, the decisions that need to be taken may be based on the criteria shown in Figure 3.2.

These criteria are explained in detail in the rest of the unit, and this is a brief outline of each one:

✶ *Understanding the situation fully*: if you do not fully understand the environment or situation you are working in, you may make incorrect or inaccurate decisions. It might be that the situation is quite complex or unfamiliar, in which case additional research may be required to help you understand and appreciate the situation better.

✶ *Searching for information related to the problem*: when you are searching for information about the problem, you need to establish what sources you need. If, for example, the problem concerns inefficiencies in a payroll system, you may have to speak to staff in the finance department and human resources department and examine documentation and procedures relating to the payroll system.

✶ *Establishing sources of information and their reliability*: once sources have been identified, you need to check whether or not the information gathered is reliable. One way to ensure this is to compare (or 'triangulate') the information source with that of another/others. By checking against other sources of information, you should be able

FACTORS TO CONSIDER IN THE DECISION-MAKING PROCESS
- Making sure that the situation is understood fully
- Cosider any other factors that need to be considered, including constraints
- Explaining the decision to others
- Analyse the information
- Searching for information related to the problem
- Select the information to be used
- Establishing sources of information and their reliability
- Identifying alternatives
- Justifying the decision
- Making the decision
- Identifying gaps in any knowledge that cannot be filled

FIGURE 3.2 *Criteria involved in the decision-making process* to guarantee the consistency and reliability of the information.

* *Identifying gaps in your knowledge*: if gaps exist in your knowledge, you might have to spend longer researching the problem and finding information to help you understand it. One way you could overcome this difficulty is to ask somebody else who does understand the problem to assist you. For example, if a company has requested a custom-made piece of software to be developed for their new system and you cannot provide this yourself, you could ask somebody to develop the software for you, but you would need to ensure that the level of expertise and quality of service are maintained.

* *Other factors and constraints*: as you work through a problem-solving exercise, you might find that other factors need to be considered, some of which could constrain the proposed solution. For example, a company may have asked for a new computerised system and specialist software for their finance department. However, no training has been discussed or agreed – so how will the users know how to operate the new system? This could be considered to be a constraint because additional costs, time and possibly resources may be required.

* *Selecting the information*: the information you select for a problem-solving activity must be appropriate, valid, current and authentic. There is no point in basing a decision on hearsay; you must have accurate information to support your decision.

* *Analysing the information*: sometimes information analysis is simply a process of elimination – because an option does not meet the specified criteria, it can be ignored. Information analysis, however, is usually more complex than this, and this complexity will depend on the size and nature of the problem. You will need to ensure that all options are fully addressed and fully justified before making a final decision.

* *Identifying alternatives*: identifying alternative solutions to the problem is considered to be good practice: it shows you have applied some thought to the problem and to the decisions you made in arriving at your final choice. Alternative solutions may be based on varying costs, specifications, resources or time frames. The solution you choose should be the best option of the alternatives available.

* *Making and justifying the decision, and explaining it to others*: when you make and justify your decision, this should be the result of extensive research and of an analysis of all the facts available. Your decision should then be communicated to the end-user(s) in an appropriate format, such as a business report.

To ensure you make the right decision, ask yourself these questions:

* Has the problem been fully investigated?
* Has adequate time been allocated to the decision-making process?

Think it over...

In small groups of three or four, collect information and carry out research that will enable you to make an informed decision based on the following scenario.

Scenario: You have been asked by your parents to organise a weekend trip away in the UK. Your parents have assigned this task to you, as you always moan about their destination choices and spend most of the holiday in a bad mood.

Using the decision-making stages listed, produce a table addressing each of the points. When you reach the last stage 'Making and justifying the decision, and explaining it to others', give a presentation to the rest of the class, identifying your destination choice, activities, accommodation and cost.

Knowledge check

List four factors that should be considered in the decision-making process.

* Are there adequate resources available to support any decisions I must make?
* Have I considered alternative solutions and on what grounds have I rejected them in favour of the actual working solution?
* Is there adequate documentation to satisfy the decisions I made during the solution specification process?

3.3 Understanding the situation

To arrive at the right decision, you often have to go through a methodical process of problem-solving. There are certain things you will need to think through in order to gain a better understanding of the situation, and this will allow you to make a more informed decision. The things you will need to address include the following:

* What exactly is it you have to decide?
* Are there different viewpoints?
* How does the decision compare with similar ones you may have made already?
* Are there variations from time to time or place to place?
* How long have you got to decide?
* What resources are at you disposal?

Trying to understand the problem is half the battle in overcoming it. If you know exactly what decisions need to be made, the process of trying to solve the problem will become more apparent.

What exactly do you have to decide?

The following activity is designed to get you thinking about actions that are taken as a result of making and carrying out a certain decision.

When you are trying to make a decision there might be alternatives or different viewpoints you need to consider. These viewpoints may arise from other people who suggest alternative options or they might arise from further research.

> **Think it over...**
>
> In small groups, consider the following decisions:
>
> Shall I take the bus or walk to college?
>
> Shall I do my assignment or go out with my mates?
>
> Try to establish for each situation exactly what it is you need to decide. For each situation, weigh up the pros and cons of each course of action.

Are there different viewpoints?

When making a decision, there may be different ways of looking at the problem, and there may be different viewpoints that you have to take into consideration.

There are many ways to arrive at different viewpoints:

* by doing some research I have discovered there are four different laptops that offer the same level of functionality as the one I have found
* by speaking to my lecturer I have found an alternative way to design my website
* by watching my mentor at work I now know how to use shortcuts on my PC.

How does the decision compare with similar ones made already?

The decisions that you make may be based on similar decisions and choices you have made in the past. If, for example, you used a particular website to gather information about a certain topic area, you may be tempted to go back and use that website again to find out information for a current assignment.

Are there variations in time or place?

Decisions can be affected by time or place, and you will have to take these into account when you arrive at your solution. For example, if you are planning a trip and the train timetable has changed since you last made the journey a month ago, you might have to take a later train or use a different mode of transport.

How long have you got to decide?

Decisions can be made in milliseconds, minutes, hours, days, months and even years. Everyday we make time-framed decisions: when we cross the road we scan our environment to check for moving cars and safety conditions; we also make estimates about how long it will take to cross (do we need to run, do we need to weave between other people who are trying to cross the road?). Some decisions do need to be made in split seconds – for example, if a saucepan of water is about to boil over, we would instinctively turn down the heat or move it off the heat. If a programme we want to watch is just about to start, we would instinctively change the channel to watch it. Other decisions, however, require thought processes rather than instinct.

What resources are at your disposal?

Resources play a big role in some of the decisions we make, and the sooner resources are identified and put at your disposal, the sooner the decision-making process can begin. Resources will vary depending on the type of decision that has to be made. For example, the resources required to plan a birthday party might include a function room, catering facilities, invitations and a party co-ordinator, etc. The resources required to complete an assignment might include books, the Internet and access to organisational information, etc.

Theory into practice

You have been asked to take part in a study that will examine the recreational activities of teenagers. The study will involve you identifying what you do in the evenings, at weekends and during non-term time and comparing your findings with other people taking part in the study.

The study will be confined to your class. You need to think about four or five recreational activities that you do and try and address the following questions that may affect your choice of activity:

* On what basis is your decision to do one recreational activity rather than another based?
* Is your activity confined to a certain time or place, or are there variations?
* How long does it take you to decide whether or not to do the activity? Is there any planning involved?
* What resources do you need, for example your friends, money, etc.?

When you have addressed all of these points, the information can be collected from the rest of the class and put together as a recreational yearbook. Class members can read out certain extracts to the group to see if anybody can guess who does what, and when.

3.4 Sources of information

You should only arrive at a decision when you are in possession of all the facts. Without this information, the accuracy and validity of any decisions you make may be distorted. To ensure you have access to these facts, therefore, you should ask yourself the following questions:

* what do I need to know
* what relevant knowledge do I already have
* what are the gaps in my knowledge and can they be filled
* what information do I already have access to
* where will any additional information come from
* how will I evaluate sources of information to ensure that content is reliable?

If you work your way through these questions, you should be able to establish if there are any gaps in your existing knowledge and, therefore, whether you need to undertake further investigations to acquire more information and where this information will come from.

What do I need to know?

To find the answer to this question, try asking some more questions. Produce a list of all the questions you need to answer. You will probably add extra questions as you go deeper into the problem, but the initial list will give you a framework.

Type your list of questions into a word-processing package. You can add notes under each question as you find out the information.

There are some techniques you can use to identify the key questions that have to be answered before a problem can be solved.

Brainstorming

This is done in a small group and everyone contributes any ideas that seem at all relevant. The important thing is for everyone to agree to stick to the one rule, which is that no-one makes any comments on any of the suggestions, however odd they may seem. This allows ideas to develop and flow. Sometimes one person will contribute a really wild idea, but that thought gets other people thinking and then they may come up with more useful ones.

One way to run a brainstorming session is to give everyone 'post-it' notes on which they write their ideas. When each person writes down and reads out an idea, the note is then stuck on a large sheet of paper or a wall panel. At the end of the session the notes can be moved around and clustered into themes. These themes can then be reworded as questions.

Spider diagrams (semantic maps)

Get a large sheet of paper and in the centre draw an image or circle that represents the problem. Draw branches off this to represent the different aspects of the problem that you need to explore. Write key words on the lines. At the end of each line draw extra lines to represent aspects of that part of the problem. If you can see things that relate to each other then link them with lines.

Using colours and images helps to bring the diagram alive. When you have finished, you should be able to write down the questions that you need to answer.

FIGURE 3.3 *Choosing a mobile phone – a spider diagram*

> **Think it over...**
>
> Suppose you are thinking of applying for a degree course in Information and Communication Technology. There are hundreds of courses spread across many different universities. You need to whittle them down to six for your UCAS application.
>
> Draw a spider diagram to help you think about what you need to know each course or university to help you make that decision.
>
> 1 List the important questions that you need to ask.
> 2 Compare your list of questions to those of other students.
> 3 Have you left any questions out?
> 4 Would you expect everyone to ask the same questions?

What relevant knowledge do I already have?

You already have a large amount of knowledge, but sometimes you do not recognise the relevance of what you know to the problem in hand. Look at your list of questions again, and this time ask yourself 'Do I know anything at all about this?'

You may decide that you know someone who seems to know a lot about the subject, or you recall having read something about it in a magazine. Add these notes under the relevant question in your list. These may be pointers to the answers rather than the answers themselves, but they are very useful starting points for further investigation.

What are the gaps in my knowledge?

You should soon see where the gaps are in your list. They will probably fall into one of these categories:

* you have some information although you are not quite sure about it and need to check
* you do not have the information you need, but you know where to find it or who to ask
* you have no information at all, as yet.

What information do I already have access to?

You can get information from a wide variety of sources, including:

* books
* documents
* magazines and newsletters
* newspapers
* maps
* pictures
* photographs
* audio
* television and video
* emails and discussion groups
* databases, spreadsheets and other computer files
* websites
* other people.

Go through your list of questions and list the sources of information that you can easily find. For example, if you know that you already have a book with some relevant information in it then add its title to your list of sources.

Primary and secondary sources

You need to distinguish between two types of sources of information:

* primary sources of information are the original documents or first-hand reports
* secondary sources of information are summaries and accounts which have been put together from primary sources.

For example, if you see a live news report on the television, which shows an event as it actually happens, then you are viewing a primary source. But if you see a reporter describing what happened after the event then you are watching a secondary source. Similarly, a history text book is a secondary source, based on the primary sources which were the original documents and objects from the period of time when the events occurred.

The problem is that when you use a secondary source you have to judge how accurate the information is. All secondary sources interpret the primary sources to some extent, however careful they are to be as objective as possible.

You may decide that the information you have is all from a secondary source and you would like to look at the primary sources. On the other hand, the author of secondary source may be an acknowledged expert in the subject and you feel you can trust them to give you unbiased information.

> **Think it over...**
>
> Go back to your list of questions about possible degree courses in ICT.
>
> 1 What knowledge do you have already?
> 2 What are the gaps in your knowledge?
> 3 What information can you get hold of easily?
> 4 Do you have any primary sources, for example, the UCAS handbook or current university students?
> 5 What would be the secondary sources?

Where will any additional information come from?

You now need to work out how to answer the questions that you have no information on, or how to get the detailed information for questions where your knowledge is rather sketchy. There are three main collections of knowledge that you can use, and you are advised to try all of them:

* libraries – librarians are highly skilled at tracking down information so do ask them for help

* experts – it is very useful if you can identify a few people who know a great deal about the subject. They may be knowledgeable through their work, or they may have a strong leisure interest, or they may just be clever. Most people are flattered if you ask their views and opinions so do not be afraid to ask for advice.

* the Internet – this offers both the huge resources of the Web itself, and also access to other people through email, discussion groups, online chat, newsgroups etc. See below for some ideas on how to use the Web effectively as a source of information.

Using the Web to find information

To use the Web effectively you need to learn how to use search engines. A search engine can search a particular site or search the whole of the Web. In both cases you enter a criterion of the search – this is usually one or more keywords. Most search engines also offer you an advanced search, where you can add extra criteria and so narrow down the search. Some search engines, such as Ask Jeeves, allow you to ask a question in normal English.

The best known search engines are Google (www.google.com), Ask Jeeves (www.ask.com) and Yahoo (www.yahoo.com). They all have UK versions (www.google.co.uk, www.ask.co.uk, www.uk.yahoo.com) which allow you to restrict your search to UK sites.

> **Think it over...**
>
> You may be surprised at how many results are listed from a search of the Web. For example, if you want to find University courses in ICT you could try each of these searches. The figures refer to the number of results produced when this was attempted with the normal Google search.
>
> * Search for **Information and Communication Technology** - over 85 million results. This gives any page which has all three words on it, but the words are not necessarily next to each other.
>
> * Search for **"Information and Communication Technology"** (including the speech marks) - over 800,000 results. This gives any web page which has the exact phrase on it.
>
> * Search for University **"Information and Communication Technology"** - nearly 400,000 results.
>
> If you use Google.co.uk rather than Google.com you will be offered the option of selecting pages from the UK.
>
> * Search for Degree **"Information and Communication Technology"** in the UK version and click on Pages from the UK - 69,000 results.
>
> Although you have reduced the number of results to well under one thousandth of the original, this is still a very large number.

Rather than doing a general search of the Web it is often easier to start at a portal or reference site and just search that. Here are some important portal and reference sites:

www.direct.gov.uk – for all UK Government services

www.ucas.com – for University courses in the UK

www.rdn.ac.uk – the Resource Discovery Network, mainly for degree students but also helpful at A Level

www.biography.com – for biographies of 25,000 people, worldwide

news.google.co.uk – the latest news from hundreds of sources

www.historyworld.net – for historical facts

www.vlib.org.uk - the WWW Virtual Library, for almost anything

www.wikipedia.org – the online encyclopaedia that has been built by its readers.

You should build up your own collection of useful portal sites.

> **Key term**
>
> A *portal site* is a website that has little content of its own, but contains many links to other useful sites.

As you gather information you should add notes about it to your list of questions.

You should also give full details of each source, selected from the following lists:

* printed materials – title, author, publisher, date of publication, page reference; you should also note where you saw source and how you can find it again

* other media – name of CD/DVD, title, date and channel of broadcast, title and source of photographs and other images

* experts – name, address, phone, email; you should note how you made the initial contact and how you can contact them again. Before you give their details, you must ask their permission as they may not be happy to have their personal information widely distributed.

* electronic materials – website address, email address.

FIGURE 3.4 *DirectGov is the UK Government's portal site for public services*

FIGURE 3.5 *The Google search engine*

FIGURE 3.6 *The Google advanced search option*

How will I evaluate sources of information to ensure that content is reliable?

You should always ask yourself whether the information you have found, from both primary and secondary sources, is correct. People can give you misleading information either because they want to mislead you, or simply by mistake. You can judge the source of the information as well as the content to decide whether you can rely on it.

Is the information appropriate?

You should check whether the information is appropriate for the problem you are trying to solve. It is easy to be captivated by interesting, but irrelevant facts.

You should check whether the information answers one or more of your questions, even if only partially. You should also try to assess whether it examines the problem in enough depth. You may need to note the source and then continue to look for better sources.

Is the information valid?

You should always check whether the information is a primary or secondary source before deciding whether it is valid. Secondary sources may have interpreted the facts incorrectly, or may not have gone to the right primary sources. You must also be aware that some information is deliberately presented in order to persuade you to take up a point of view, so may not give equal weighting to all the facts.

It is very difficult to decide whether a piece of information is true, even when you do have access to primary sources. If several people witness a crime being committed they will give different accounts in court of the event and may even contradict each other, although they are all trying to tell the truth. The jury has to decide what really happened, and take into account where each person was standing at the time, what they were doing and even their personality.

You need to be aware of these kinds of discrepancies and try to gather as much information as possible so you can cross-check one statement against another.

Is the information current?

You can check whether the information is up to date, by finding out whether a date is given anywhere. Books give the date of original publication plus the date at which it was revised. Newspapers and magazines always give the day or month when they were published. In the case of a webpage you may be able to see when it was last updated.

Of course, old information may still be important and useful, but if you think that later material is available then you should try to find it.

Is the source of the information authentic?

When you buy a copy of a national newspaper, such as The Independent, you can be reasonably sure that you are reading the real thing. But that is not necessarily true of web sites, and a number of scams have been associated with counterfeit sites. A similar problem has occurred in the past with primary historical sources which have turned out to be forgeries.

You can check a website in a number of ways.

* Look at the website address – if it ends with .edu or .ac.uk then you know that it comes from a reputable academic institution in the US or UK. If it ends with .gov.uk then it is a genuine UK governmental organisation.

* Check the Contacts or About Us page – it should give real world contact details, such as an address and phone number. Look for details of the people involved in the site, and do a web search on some of the names for more information about them.

* Do other sites link to the site? You can check this by entering the website address in a search engine (you must put speech marks around it) and see if other sites refer to it. Are they ones that you can trust?

You can check the details of a book or magazine like this:

* look for the name and address of the publisher, and then check the publisher's website (do remember that some people and organisations publish their own material and they will not use a well-known publisher)

* look for the ISBN (International Standard Book Number) allocated to any book published by a genuine publisher. Again, self-published books will probably not have an ISBN, but this does not mean that they are not genuine.

You can check the author or creator of a work several ways.

* Check whether the author's name appears somewhere. If you do not recognise the name then check it out on the Web.
* It is sometimes difficult to know whether the work is created by the named person. In the case of works of art and historical documents an expert in the field may authenticate them.
* You can check whether the item comes from a trusted source. For example, if a web page on the BBC site claims that an article has been written by a named reporter then you can be confident in its authenticity.

> **Theory into practice**
>
> There is a wide range of information sources, all of which are valuable in their own right. The use of different information sources can enrich a task, project, piece of research or decision.
>
> Using three information sources, collect information about your favourite actor/actress. You might decide to use magazine features, the Internet, newspaper articles and reviews as the basis for your investigation.
>
> Collect the information and produce a display of your findings (perhaps as a poster). Include the source of each piece of information you use. Add labels to evaluate the different sources.

> **Knowledge check**
>
> 1 What methods can be used to gather information?
> 2 To ensure you have access to all the facts before making a decision, what questions should you ask yourself?

3.5 Other factors to consider

Gathering knowledge and resources can contribute greatly to the quality and accuracy of any decisions you make, but there are occasions when information and resources are not enough. Other factors can also have an impact on the way in which you arrive at a decision:

* *Gut feelings* ('I just know that this is the right thing to do'): you have an instinct, something tells you not to do that or not to go a certain place, or not to make a certain purchase. 'Gut feelings' and instinct are often the knowledge we have learned through our past experiences, but which have become so embedded in our minds that we have forgotten how we first learned them.
* *Sentiment* ('what will others think?'): a personal belief or judgment based on feeling or emotion rather than proof or certainty; 'my opinion differs from yours'; 'what are your thoughts on the election?'
* *Emotion* ('I will never forgive myself if I make a risky decision'): how would you feel if you carried out an activity that went wrong? Would you be able to live with yourself? Was the decision against your will – you possibly thought it ethically or morally wrong?
* *Ambition* ('How will this affect my career?'): if I make the right decision, will this improve my prospects for promotion? If I get it wrong, will this harm my career?
* *Lack of knowledge* ('Do I know enough to do this?'): am I ready to make this decision? What if I do not understand something?

Sentiments such as the ones listed at the beginning of this section can play a role in any decisions you must make. You may, for example, decide against a certain course of action in case you upset somebody's feelings, or you may worry about what others may think.

> **Think it over...**
>
> In small groups, discuss an issue that might arise if you were asked to make the following ethical and moral decisions. Would you:
>
> 1 Work for a company that carried out testing on animals?
> 2 Wear leather if you were a vegetarian?
> 3 Allow a friend to copy your work and pass it off as his or her own?
> 4 Take the credit for something when you are aware that the credit belonged to somebody else?
> 5 Own up if you accidentally scratched your neighbour's car?
> 6 Admit to finding £20 in the school/college canteen?

Ambition can drive decisions: as a knowledge worker you might experiment with ideas to come up with more innovative and creative solutions that could help to advance your career. At the same time, however, you will be aware that the wrong decision may put a halt to any career options you may have.

Gaps in your knowledge might constrain the type of career you choose as a knowledge worker because you do not have the necessary skills or ability. For example, to be a web designer you might need programming skills, flair to design pages and excellent interpersonal skills to communicate with different end-users. The decisions you would need to make to fill in these gaps in your knowledge might include learning to program, attending courses and, possibly, working alongside web designers so that you can learn by watching others doing this job.

3.6 Making a decision

To help you make decisions, you will practise using spreadsheet models. Spreadsheet modelling is useful because data can be extracted from the original data set and placed into a table, used as a basis for further calculations or used for forecasting and prediction purposes. All of these actions can aid the decision-making process and provide the user with better informed decisions.

The models you create will be checked for correctness and will be evaluated against certain variables to ensure that the information provided meets the specified requirements. These requirements will include such things as cost effectiveness, efficiency and quality issues.

Throughout the modelling process the decisions you take will need to be fully justified and supported by documentation and recommendations. Finally, you will be expected to evaluate the model(s) you have created and to cross-reference your method of solution against the original objectives.

Spreadsheets

Spreadsheets present a clear and consistent way of understanding and interpreting data. Data can be keyed into a spreadsheet and the spreadsheet can be stored as a skeleton template so that further additions and updates can be added when necessary. Provided you have set up formulae on the spreadsheet, new data can be incorporated and updated easily to provide the user with current facts and figures. Spreadsheets can be used as a modelling tool to provide users with a range of features to enable them to:

* produce and display numerical, graphical and statistical data such as:
    - sales forecasts (see Figure 3.7)
    - profits and losses
    - general expenditure (see Figure 3.8)
    - wage and salary information
    - distribution facts
* forecast information
* calculate information
* predict alternative outcomes and behaviour under different conditions
* analyse information
* automate procedures.

FIGURE 3.7 Sample spreadsheet to calculate and forecast information

FIGURE 3.8 Sample monthly expenditure spreadsheet

FIGURE 3.9 Examples of the charts and graphs offered by spreadsheets

Theory into practice

Using either a spreadsheet or a database, design a small system to meet one of the following user requirements:

1 A system a hire shop could use to store information about DVDs and videos it has available for hire. Your system should include:

* customer details
* details of DVD/video titles
* rental status.

2 A stock control system template for a vehicle-repair shop that will automatically calculate stock levels and reorder levels. Your system should include:

* the period January to June
* stock items (fan belts, spark plugs, wheel nuts, fuses and tyres)
* a minimum stock level requirement of 60 items
* an indicator to show when stock items must be reordered

Your designs should be clear and fully functional. All the data you use should come from you and should be substantial enough to demonstrate the functionality of each system.

A spreadsheet that contains large amounts of data may not be easy to interpret. You can, therefore, use the graphical features offered by a spreadsheet to present data in a more visual way. Some spreadsheet applications, for example, have built-in chart and graphic facilities to provide the user with a visual interpretation of the data (see Figure 3.9).

Spreadsheet functions

There are a number of functions that can be used to model spreadsheets. These include:

* SUMIF
* Average
* Count.

	A	B	C	D	E	F	G	H	I	J
1	**Sales and commission for January 2003**									
2										
3		January		Commission 1.5%						
4		£		£						
5	Part A	12,000		180						
6	Part B	3,400		51						
7	Part C	4,900		74						
8	Part D	6,100		92						
9	Part E	7,200		108						
10	Part F	3,900		59						
11	Part G	6,890		10						
12	Part H	7,970		12						
13										
14	Calculated commission for part sales that have exceeded £5,000 in January									£602.40

=SUMIF(B5:B12, "> 5000",D5:D12)

FIGURE 3.10 *SUMIF*

In this section we will look at the SUMIF function. Spreadsheet functions can sometimes be quite complex. However they are quite necessary in order to fully manipulate spreadsheet datasets. In section 3.12 the basics of a spreadsheet are discussed, so you should ensure that you understand how to set up a worksheet and that you can perform basic calculations before you start to use some of the more complex functions.

SUMIF adds up the cells you have selected according to the criteria you have set. SUMIF, therefore, works like this:

SUMIF = range, criteria, sum range

* The *range* is the range of cells that you want to apply the criteria to.
* The *criteria* are used to determine which cells you want to add up. A criterion can be in the form of a number, an expression or text that defines which cells will be added. For example, criteria can be expressed as 40, "40", ">40", "widgets".
* The *sum range* are the cells you want to sum.

The cells in sum range are totalled only if their corresponding cells in the range match the criteria (see Figure 3.10). If sum range is omitted, the cells in the range are totalled.

3.7 Computer modelling

When you practise using spreadsheet models, you must bear in mind that decisions based on these models will only be as good as the models themselves. Before you put your trust in a model, therefore, whether your own or someone else's, you must make sure it is correct:

* is the logic it uses correct
* are the data formats appropriate
* is the syntax of the formulae correct
* are the cell references correct?

It's a good idea to look at a range of existing models; for example, financial models that could illustrate profit, loss and cash flow, and decision models that could perform forecasts for the future based on a given data set and certain rules and conditions. By using different models and evaluating them you can get an overview of a range of tools and techniques that can be used to manipulate spreadsheets. Models can evaluated in a number of ways, for example:

* what processes or scenarios are being modelled
* what does the model actually do
* how well does it do it
* could it be improved
* which variables can be input
* what outputs are identified
* what decisions could be made when using the model?

Theory into practice

You work in a large stationery shop. Your role is to help the supervisor with the stock take and the reordering of stationery supplies. Although you are just a trainee at present, it is expected that you will be promoted to a supervisory role within six months.

Part of the supervisor's responsibilities is to try to identify what supplies will be in demand over a four-week period. At certain times of the year it is quite easy to do this – for example, between August and September the demand for 'back to school' stationery is very high. This is also the case in January when students return to school and college after the Christmas break.

In order to assist you in your decision-making process about what stock items should be ordered, the manager of the shop has started to design a spreadsheet based on a budget of £250 (see Figure 3.11).

	B	C	D	E
1		Stock budget		
2				
3	Item	Price	Number	Cost
4	Ring binder	0.79	0.00	0.00
5	A4 Pad	1.25	0.00	0.00
6	A5 Pad	1.05	0.00	0.00
7	Pack 10 clear wallets	2.15	0.00	0.00
8				
9	Pak of 5 folders	1.79	0.00	0.00
10	Pack of 4 pens	0.99	0.00	0.00
11	Stationary set	3.75	0.00	0.00
12	Pack of 3 ruled pads	2.00	0.00	0.00
13				
14	Pack of 3 storage boxes	3.45	0.00	0.00
15				
16				
17	Enter the number of unit stationary items			
18	required to make up the £250 budget			

C4*D4
Formulas need to be added for the cost column

A total column needs to be added to check that the cost falls within the £250 budget

FIGURE 3.11 *Stationery items: sample spreadsheet*

1 Look at the sample spreadsheet and complete the model using various combinations of stationery item quantities.

2 The spreadsheet that has been set up by the manager is incomplete: formulae should be included to total up each stationery item, and a Total Cost needs to be included to check that the items ordered falls within the £250 parameter.

3 Once the spreadsheet has been set up, project the information visually in a graph of your choice.

4 Identify other modelling techniques that can be used with this spreadsheet.

> **Knowledge check**
>
> 1. What is meant by the term 'spreadsheet model'?
> 2. Identify a range of spreadsheet models.
> 3. Why is modelling useful in spreadsheet design and manipulation?

3.8 Using a model to consider alternatives

When you have designed your own model(s), you need to ensure that they are working correctly and that they meet the original design requirements. You may find that, although a solution has been provided, alternatives exist that may be more cost-effective, labour saving or resourceful, for example. Therefore, you will need to devise a system for scrutinising and analysing your model. The system you devise should show that you have addressed, and answered, the following questions:

* Does the decisions I have decided upon produce the best results?
* What alternatives have I looked at?
* What makes the alternatives not as suitable as the solution I have chosen?
* What, if anything, does the model I have chosen *not* take into account – what are its limitations?
* What might be the impact of these limitations or constraints in the short and long term?

> **Think it over...**
>
> Modelling provides a framework on which to base decisions, make prediction and forecasts. What would happen if there were no modelling tools available? How would you be able to make good decisions?

Justifying the decision

Once you have developed and tested your model, you must produce supporting documentation that shows the key features of model and that demonstrates how your design meets the original aims and objectives.

The key features of a model could describe what the model does, how it does it, the benefits and impact of using the model and how it can be adapted in the future. Your model may change over time depending on what your expectations are and how it performs under certain conditions. Your initial aims and objectives may have been met by the model. However, as things change, the model may require updating to accommodate these new requirements.

> ✱ **REMEMBER!**
>
> As you work through the decision-making process, keep a record of your processes and results, so that the information will be readily available when you come to write up your report or give a presentation on your decisions and recommendations.

Reporting it to others

You should write a short report that outlines the original problem, aims and objectives, and the final decision you made. This will focus your thoughts in a very structured and systematic way. You could add graphs and charts to the report to provide a visual overview of your model. If the model is quite complex to use, it might also be appropriate to design a user guide to help the reader understand why you have used a particular model and how the model has been created.

Your documentation should also include any recommendations you wish to make. These will help the end-user in understanding and appreciating the complexity of the model. Any recommendations you make should include:

* a summary of the current situation
* your sources and any alternatives you have considered

* other factors that you took into consideration
* the methods you used to reach your decision
* the decision itself
* a justification of your decision, supported by evidence of the decision-making process you went through.

Evaluating a model

To confirm that your model is successful, you must decide whether or not it meets the specified requirements. To do this, you must assess:

* how well your model has performed
* the extent to which the model has helped you in making the right decision
* what else you would like the model to do
* if your model need extending and, if so, how?

To help you in your evaluation, you could use a checklist such as the one shown in Table 3.4, which uses a brief for a toy company as an example.

REQUIREMENTS	MET? YES/NO		
The spreadsheet can display a breakdown of the sales for each toy over a six-month period (monetary and quantity based)			
Average sales can be calculated for each month			
Trends in sales can be identified over the period			
If a new toy was introduced on to the market you would be able to forecast a selling price for the next six-month period based on the average selling price for the month plus 10 per cent			
The spreadsheet can display a breakdown of the sales for each toy over a six-month period (monetary and quantity based)			
Functionality and appearance: * Do the formulae all work? * Are more formulae needed? * Comments:			
Does the model need extending?	Within 6 months	Within a year	Within 1–3 years
Comment on the way in which the model will need extending:			
Final comments:			

TABLE 3.4 *Evaluation checklist*

> **Theory into practice**
>
> When you develop a model to meet a user or business requirement, there may be alternative models that you could use that would give you access to different information, or allow you to make different decisions.
>
> For the model that you are developing to meet the requirements of this unit, outline two other models that could be used. Draw up a table to compare your model and the two alternative models in terms of:
>
> * *functionality* – how well will the model work? Compare its features, such as automatic calculations, formulas and functions
> * *usability* – how easy and practical are the models
> * *practicality* – how useful are the models in terms of aiding the end-user in the decision-making process?

3.9 ICT skills

This section is designed to provide you with an overview of types of application software. You will not be using applications to design and build working models and templates from scratch. However, you may be expected to amend models and templates. This section, therefore, provides you with basics on how to address tasks, and carry out processing activities to enable you to improve initial designs and evaluate their performance. It will also enable you to advance into more complex tasks associated with modelling tools and techniques as identified in section 3.6.

Carrying out spreadsheet modelling tasks

In order to support you in your spreadsheet modelling, you will learn about a range of tools and techniques you can incorporate into your own designs. This section, therefore, provides you with examples and screen shots of some of the more popular tools and techniques used in spreadsheet modelling.

Entering and editing data

Cells in a spreadsheet are identified by a series of letters and numbers. The letters identify the columns and the numbers the rows. To enter data into a spreadsheet, click on the appropriate cell (for example A1, B3, C2, etc.) (Figure 3.12).

In the example in Figure 3.13 you can see that the data entered in cell E5 (1888) also appears in the Formula bar at the top of the screen. If you wanted to change the data for cell E5, you would click on that cell and key in the new data, or key in the data directly on the Formula bar.

Revised data can be typed into any one of these two places.

FIGURE 3.12 *Entering and editing data*

Formatting data

In the Formatting menu, there a number of criteria you can select to format your spreadsheet. The examples provided in this section will look at the formatting of cells and conditional formatting features (see Figure 3.13). It is suggested that you experiment with the other format options on your spreadsheet when you do your own modelling.

Formatting cells

You can format individual cells, rows, columns or entire sheets. Here we will focus on the formatting of cells.

Using the **Cells…** option on the **Format** menu drop-down list, **Number** function, it is easy to select data values and set them to two decimal places, as shown in these three easy steps.

Step one (Figure 3.14): enter the data to be formatted.

Step two (Figure 3.15): format the data.

Step three (Figure 3.16): data is formatted. There are other formatting functions you can use in the Format Cells dialogue box, including Alignment, Font, Border, Patterns and Protection (Figure 3.17 shows the options available if the **Border** tab is selected).

Conditional formatting

This function allows you to select the type of formatting wish to apply to certain data, and under certain conditions. On the **Menu** bar, select: **Format, Conditional Formatting.**

FIGURE 3.13 *Formatting data*

	A	B	C	D	E
1	Enter and edit spreadsheet data				
2					
3		Monetary sales per quarter 2004			
4		Q1	Q2	Q3	Q4
5	Type 1	1367	2746	2510	1888
6	Type 2	2435	1003	1890	2093
7	Type 3	1675	3112	2871	3155
8	Type 4	2665	2900	2673	2146

Enter the data to be formatted

FIGURE 3.14 *Entering the data to be formatted*

Select 'number' from the format menu, and click up or down for the amount of decimal places – in this e.g. '2'

FIGURE 3.15 *Formatting the data*

Enter the data to be formatted

FIGURE 3.16 *Formatted data*

FIGURE 3.18 *Conditional formatting*

FIGURE 3.17 *Format Cells dialogue box, Border tab selected*

The Conditional Formatting dialogue box is displayed. In the example in Figure 3.18, all data between the value of 2000 and 3000 have been emboldened. To do this, once the conditions have been set in the Conditional Formatting dialogue box, click on: **Format** to display the Format Cells dialogue box where you can chose the required formatting.

Analysing and interpreting data (e.g. filters)

If you apply a filter to a spreadsheet, this will allow you to focus on a particular section of data – screening off the rest of the spreadsheet. On the Menu bar, select: **Data, Filter, AutoFilter** (Figure 3.19).

By clicking on the down arrow at the side of the Total cell (see Figure 3.20), you can apply a filter to the Total column and therefore select which totals you want to view – in this case those for 8738 relating to Type 1 items.

Sort

The Sort function allows you to sort information in ascending or descending order. On the **Menu** bar, select: **Data, Sort**. The Sort dialogue box is displayed (Figure 3.21). You can select which data you want to sort by clicking on each criteria – **Sort by, Then by, Then by**.

For example, you could sort student enrolment information alphabetically by surname as show in Table 3.5.

Using formulae and functions

Formulae and functions can be used to manipulate data within a spreadsheet and also to take away some of the repetitive tasks involved with calculating and analysing data. Formulae and functions provide you with a ready-made toolkit that will allow you to develop a worksheet into a working financial, statistical, business or decision-based model. Formulae can be set up and then copied to save time and also to reduce errors within the spreadsheet (Figure 3.22). By using cell referencing you can analyse spreadsheet data in almost any way that you may require.

FIGURE 3.19 *Applying a filter*

FIGURE 3.20 *Selecting a filter*

FIGURE 3.21 *The Sort dialogue box*

Validating and checking data

There are a number of ways that data can be validated and checked within a spreadsheet. If an incorrect formula has been inserted, an error message may be displayed (Figure 3.23).

If you need to track which variables have been used in a calculation Formula auditing (Figure 3.24) and Trace precedents can be used to map the individual cells. Formulae can also be evaluated using the formula auditing feature to

FIGURE 3.22 *Example of a spreadsheet formula*

Unsorted
Student enrolment information

Surname	First name	Enrolment number
James	Stewart	SJ/1267OP
Harrison	Charlotte	CH/5374LP
Michaels	John	JM/2900GL
Davids	Rebecca	RD/6729HN
Smyth	Pippa	PS/2773BN
Peterson	Jack	JP/7002LS
Morris	Joan	JM/3544NM
Jacobs	Mary	MJ/1003RT

Sorted
Student enrolment information

Surname	First name	Enrolment number
Davids	Rebecca	RD/6729HN
Harrison	Charlotte	CH/5374LP
Jacobs	Mary	MJ/1003RT
James	Stewart	SJ/1267OP
Michaels	John	JM/2900GL
Morris	Joan	JM/3544NM
Peterson	Jack	JP/7002LS
Smyth	Pippa	PS/2773BN

TABLE 3.5 *Alphabetically sorted surnames*

identify cells that have been used in any given calculations.

Validation of a spreadsheet model can also include inputting reminders of values to be entered (Figure 3.26).

FIGURE 3.24 *Formula auditing toolbar*

FIGURE 3.23 *Data validation error message*

FIGURE 3.25 *An example of formula auditing*

UNIT 3: THE KNOWLEDGE WORKER

FIGURE 3.26 *Using a reminder*

Presenting information

Graphs and charts provide a more visual overview of any data you have generated in your spreadsheet. If you follow the steps in the Chart Wizard (select: the **Chart Wizard** icon on the Toolbar) (Figure 3.27), there are a number of graphs and charts you can create.

Pie charts

Each segment of the pie chart in Figure 3.28 represents a percentage of games consoles sold for each month from August to January. The smallest segment is 6 per cent for August and the largest is 35 per cent for December.

FIGURE 3.27 *Chart Wizard, Step 1*

Bar graphs

Each bar on the bar graph in Figure 3.29 represents a type of games console ranging from A to D. The bar graph identifies how many of each console was sold each month.

FIGURE 3.29 *Bar graph*

Line graph

The line graph in Figure 3.30 clearly plots the sales of each console from August to January. It is evident that Type A console is the best seller and that Type C console is the worst seller. From this graph it is

FIGURE 3.30 *Line graph*

also clear that in August, September and January sales were very similar for Types B, C and D.

Scatter graph

Scatter graphs (Figure 3.31) are best used when there is a lot of numerical data that requires plotting to identify a pattern in the data. The scatter graph in Figure 3.31 shows the pattern of sales for each month, 1–6. In August it clearly shows that all four games console types had similar sales figures. However in December these sales are quite different.

FIGURE 3.31 *Scatter graph*

	A	B	C	D	E	F	G	H	I
1	Sales forecast spreadsheet January–June 2005								
2									
3		January	February	March	April	May	June	July	Aug
4		£	£	£	£	£	£	£	£
5	Part A	12,000	5,600	4,800	4,700	5,000	11,900	11,200	16,800
6	Part B	3,400	3,900	1,200	3,400	4,678	6,900	2,578	3222.5

FIGURE 3.32 *An example of automatic calculation*

and how the techniques are incorporated into their own designs.

> **Knowledge check**
> 1 What can a filter do?
> 2 How can you validate a spreadsheet?
> 3 Identify three types of spreadsheet model.
> 4 Why is modelling so important?

Modifying spreadsheet models to take account of requirements

Spreadsheet models can be modified to take into account different requirements or needs. For example on a 'sales forecast spreadsheet', a change in the market might impact on the price of an item. Therefore more or less might have to be sold to break-even. By changing a single variable, such as increasing the cost of an item, the entire model will also change and adapt to the new increase.

If a calculation was used to forecast August's sales, based on a 25 per cent increase on July's figures (Figure 3.26), a change in the July forecast figure would then subsequently alter the forecasting for any other months using the July figures as a basis (Figure 3.32).

ICT skills are skills that you acquire, learn and develop when you use certain applications, hardware and software. In terms of software, ICT skills are judged by the competency of the end-user in interacting with the menus and toolbars

Word processing

Word processing software can support you in the preparation and writing up all sorts of documents. Depending upon the nature of your task, it can be used to:

* import data from other applications
* format documents
* creat document layouts
* check documents.

Importing data from other applications

There are a number of ways that data can be imported from other applications into a word processed document, such as Word. You can, for instance, import a chart created in Excel.

With the Word document open on screen, position the cursor in the document where you want the chart to appear. Now open Excel and open the file that contains the chart. Select the entire chart by clicking in a white space outside the plotted chart area. Click on the **Copy** button and switch back to the Word document by clicking in its button on the taskbar at the bottom of the

FIGURE 3.34 Inserting a file

FIGURE 3.35 Insert File dialogue box

screen. With the Word document on screen, click on the **Paste** button and the chart will be imported into the document.

You can also insert files into a Word document by selecting **Insert** from the **Menu** bar, then clicking on **File…** (Figure 3.34). This will bring the Insert File dialogue box on screen (Figure 3.35). In the **Look in** box, select the file you want to import (click on the down arrow at the side of this box to view all the files). So that you can view all files and not just Word files, make sure **All Files** is selected in the **Files of type** box. When you have located the correct file, click on it, then on **Insert**. The file will be imported into the Word document.

Formatting documents that have been imported

There are a number of documents that can be formatted and imported into word processing software such as Word. Documents or files can include:

* tables
* spreadsheets
* graphics
* data sets used for mail merging
* scanned images
* drawings
* downloaded material.

For some documents, the format might have to be changed so that they can be opened into Word format. Layout and sizing changes may also have to be addressed to ensure that it is legible to view or read.

Creating document layouts

You can create tables in Word. To produce a table with a fixed number of columns and rows, on the **Menu** bar, select: **Table, Insert, Table** (Figure 3.36). The Insert Table dialogue box is displayed (Figure 3.37).

FIGURE 3.36 *Inserting a table*

FIGURE 3.37 *Insert Table dialogue box*

Select the number of columns and rows you require in the boxes in the **Table size** pane (the other selections should be left as they are, i.e. **Fixed column width** selected and **Auto** displayed). Now click on **OK**. The table grid will appear in the document. Table 3.6 was produced this way. Once the grid had been created, the entries were added to the cells, and the cells increased in size, when necessary, to accommodate the entries.

If you want to change the appearance of the columns in a Word document, you can arrange these as two, three or four vertical columns. First, highlight the text you want to arrange in columns. Then click on the **Column** icon on the Standard toolbar (Figure 3.38). In the drop-down list, select two, three or four columns, as required.

Column icon

FIGURE 3.38 *Selecting columns*

Checking documents

There are a number of standard tools that can be used to check documents in Word, some of these include checking for spelling (**Spell check**), grammar and punctuation. Language checks can also be carried out using the translation tool and text can be converted from English to French or Spanish, for example. In addition, documents can also be previewed and checked prior to printing (**Print preview**).

POLICY NUMBERS	INITIALS	CUSTOMER SINCE	INSURANCE TYPE
ST/01/L/34849	ST	2001	L – Life
RB/02/M/74788	RB	2002	M – Motor
LD/89/H/56337	LD	1989	H – House

TABLE 3.6 *Table created by the Insert Table dialogue box method*

BENEFITS OF USING PRESENTATION SOFTWARE
- Can be easy to use
- Customise each presentation
- Can be quick to use
- Widely available
- Provides step-by-step designs
- Allows for interactivity
- Incorporates sound and images both static and moving

FIGURE 3.39 *Benefits of using presentation software*

Producing presentations

Using presentations

Good presentation skills are essential in all environments; people will have expectations of your ability to present information clearly, cohesively, relevantly and knowledgeably.

Methods and styles of presentations include:

* formal/informal
* use of ICT resources/no ICT resource use
* delivery to a wide audience/to individuals.

Formal and informal presentations

In terms of formality, a presentation will differ depending upon the environment in which it is being delivered and the intended audience. Formal presentations tend to be more structured with more time built into the planning and overall delivery. Formal presentations may also be delivered to an audience that is not known to you. This may be especially true within an organisational environment.

Formal presentations can include:

* providing feedback on a project at work
* representation at a meeting
* press release

* awards ceremony speech.

Informal presentations are more likely to be quite casual, where the presenter may talk 'ad lib' with little or no preparation. This may not always be the case, but informal presentations do encourage 'freestyle' speech.

Click to add title

Click to add subtitle

New
- Blank Presentation
- From Design Template
- From AutoContent Wizard

Blank presentation

Ways of creating a presentation slide

FIGURE 3.40 *Creating a presentation using PowerPoint®*

FIGURE 3.41 *Formatting a slide using PowerPoint®*

Informal presentations can include:

* presentation on 'new film releases' as part of your coursework
* recounting events of a holiday to a friend
* thank-you/congratulations speech to friends or family.

FIGURE 3.42 *Text and content layout variations in PowerPoint*

Styles of delivery

Presentations can be delivered in a number of ways, with or without the use of ICT, including:

* reading from cards, sheets, etc.
* free style
* using presentation software
* using aids such as flip charts, overhead transparencies (OHTs), whiteboard, etc.

Some people find it quite difficult to recall large amounts of data and information from memory when giving a presentation. They may, therefore, need a prompt to aid in the recall process. Speakers often use small index cards or a sheet of paper containing a few bullet points as a prompt.

Using ICT to produce presentations

ICT now plays a big role in the way in which presentations are delivered and in the overall quality of presentations. Software applications, such as PowerPoint, can be used for the specific purpose of delivering a professional presentation. Presentation software today can provide a number of benefits as shown in Figure 3.39.

When you use presentation software, you will learn about:

* creating and editing presentations
* formatting slides
* inserting text, pictures and charts
* importing data from other applications
* checking presentations.

Creating and editing presentations

The use of presentation software can allow you to create and edit presentations. Using software such as PowerPoint, for example, you can create professional presentation slides starting from: a **Blank Presentation** slide, a **Design Template,** or from the **AutoContent Wizard** (Figure 3.40).

Formatting slides

There are a number of ways that presentation slides can be formatted using PowerPoint. By selecting: **Format, Slide Design, Design Templates** you can apply or change a design template; choose **Colour Schemes** to apply or change the colour scheme, and **Animation Schemes** to apply or change an animation (Figure 3.41).

In addition, by selecting Format, Slide Layout, the slide can be formatted to include a variety of Text Layouts and Content Layouts (Figure 3.42). By selecting: **Slide Show, Slide Transition,** you can customise your slide show to:

* control the speed of each slide
* determine the way in which the slide appears on the screen (for example, dissolving in)

FIGURE 3.43 *Using a Text and Content Layout to insert content using PowerPoint®*

✱ automatically time the length of each slide
✱ decide how the slides are advanced.

You can also include a link to other applications on the Internet.

Inserting text, pictures and charts

Inserting text, pictures and charts on a slide can easily be achieved in PowerPoint using **Text Layouts** or **Content Layouts.** Select the layout you want to use for the slide, then click on the relevant icon to add the content you require (Figure 3.43).

Importing data from other applications

Importing data from other applications can also be carried out quite easily using a PowerPoint® presentation and selecting: Insert from the toolbar. Graphs, charts, pictures or other applications such as spreadsheets can all be integrated into a slide show (Figure 3.44).

Checking presentations

When you have completed your presentation slides, it is a good idea to check through the content to make sure that there are no spelling or grammatical errors. In addition, check that the graphics and any imported files, charts, pictures, etc. are positioned correctly. If you have used any special features, such as timings or animations, also ensure that they have been set up appropriately. When using animation and sound, make sure that these do not distract your audience from the content of the presentation.

Run through your complete presentation a least a couple of times before presenting it to your target audience

FIGURE 3.44 *Importing pictures from other applications using PowerPoint®*

Theory into practice

1. Create a short presentation using six slides. The presentation theme should be based on mobile phone technologies.
2. Within your presentation, use at least one graphic and one table or chart.
3. Use at least two formatting features to enhance your presentation.
4. Print your presentation out six slides to a page.

Knowledge check

Presentation software is an excellent way for a knowledge worker to visually communicate their thoughts and ideas.

1. Give three examples or scenarios showing when and how a knowledge worker could use presentation software.
2. What are the benefits of communicating information in a visual format?

GLOSSARY

Analogue
A physical form of information; radio waves for your FM radio are analogue.

Anchor
Labels a particular position on a web page, so that you can then jump to that position from elsewhere on the same page or from another page within the website.

Animation
A sequence of stills which, when run together, form a moving picture.

Applet
Short for application and describes a very short program, i.e. a piece of code, written for use on the world wide web.

ASCII
American Standard Code for Information Interchange. Each letter and character has a unique ASCII code in the range 0 to 127; for example, the letter M is 77.

ATX
AT is an old IBM computer that became the standard for computer cases and power supplies; ATX is an extension of the AT standard.

Audio cable
Cable with three wires which runs from the CD-ROM drive to the sound card, enabling the PC to play audio CDs through the sound card and out through speakers.

Automatically processed
Processed by computer or other technology.

Banner
An image link used to advertise a sponsor of a web site.

Bar code
An internationally recognised, machine-readable symbol widely used in a number of applications where items need to be recognised, such as supermarkets, stock control and asset management.

Bespoke
Something made for individual use or to meet individual requirements, such as a custom-made computer system.

BIOS
'Basic input output systems'; it is a computer chip which controls the computer startup process.

Bit
'Binary digit'. A bit is either on or off and is represented by '1' or '0'.

Bitmap
An image that stores each pixel (image element) as a two-dimensional grid.

Blog
(A shortened form of 'weblog') a web page that serves as a publicly accessible personal journal for an individual.

Bookmark
Add a wesbites URL (uniform resource locator) to a list of favourite sites which can then be revisited quickly, by clicking on the bookmark.

Boot sector
A sector on the disk set aside to hold programs that control the loading up of other programs, from which the system is booted up.

Broadband
A term for a higher speed internet connection for the home or small office user. The connection speed varies from 128 kbps to more than 3 Mbps, depending on the service provider. The speed is constantly increasing as technology improves; soon home internet access will be of a comparable speed to the speed of the average corporate network ten years ago.

Broadcast
A network message that is sent to everyone on the stem that is listening.

Browser
A program which lets you view web pages on the internet.

Button
A feature that looks like a button and – when you click the mouse while the cursor is positioned on it – some event happens.

Byte
8 bits = 1 byte.

Chat rooms
A method of communication provided by the internet. Users key in messages about some topic of interest which are displayed in real time on the PCs of all the users who are currently in the same chat room.

CMOS
Complementary metal-oxide semiconductor, an essential hardware part of the motherboard, which holds the BIOS, an essential software part of the motherboard.

Comma separated values (CSV)
A text file which can be used to store database records. Each field on the file is separated by a comma, and each record is separated by a carriage return. CSV files are sometimes used to transfer data between systems since they can be easily exported and imported.

Command
An instruction given to the central processor by a computer program (set of instructions).

Configure
Customise the computer system for a specific purpose.

Cookie
A text file that a web server can store on a user's hard disk when they view a page from that server.

CPU
Central processing unit, the technical term for the processor than runs the computer.

Credit card
A card allowing purchases which are added to a monthly account. A monthly statement lists all transactions, some or all of the outstanding balance must be paid.

Cross talk
Caused when electrical signals in one pair of wires create a magnetic field, which then causes a signal to flow in another pair of wires.

CRT (cathode ray tube)
The type of monitor that uses the same technology as a TV.

Data controllers
Those who control the contents, and use of, a collection of personal data. They can be any type of company or organisation, large or small, within the public or private sector.

Data subjects
The individuals to whom the personal data relates.

Debit card
A card issued by a bank allowing a person to make payments from a bank account to anyone

who can accept the card. The payments are taken more or less immediately from your bank account.

Defragmentation
Tidies up the disk, making available clusters that are no longer needed (because files have been deleted) and collecting the separate elements of fragmented files together.

Digital
This signifies the data of the computer systems as binary 0s and 1s, or as ON/OFF electrical pulses.

DIMM
Double inline memory module.

DIP
Dual inline packaging; where pins are arranged in two rows either side of the chip.

DOS
Disk Operating System.

Drag and drop
Select an object (an image or some highlighted text) by clicking on it. Then, without releasing the mouse button, drag the object using the mouse and place in the required position on the web page, where it is dropped by releasing the mouse button.

DRAM
Dynamic RAM; the cheaper RAM, but one that does need frequent refreshing – i.e. rewriting – of the data.

Dual-booting systems
Have more than one operating system installed and give the user the option as to which operating system is to be loaded and run.

DUN (dial-up networking)
An option for connecting to the internet.

E-books
Digital books designed to be viewed onscreen. E-books can contain animated video clips and audio files, animated diagrams, 360-degree stills and photographs that can be zoomed into, etc.

EIDE
Enhanced IDE – a more sophisticated version of IDE, so-called at one time because it supported a particular new technology.

Electronic Data Interchange (EDI)
A method used by businesses to transfer documents electronically over the Internet or other network.

Enclosure connector
A cable from the case to the motherboard for the reset button and various lights.

Encryption key
A secret numerical code applied to a message so it is transmitted or stored in indecipherable characters. The message can only be read after it has been reconstructed through the use of a 'matching key'.

Encryption software
Software which scrambles message transmissions.

ERD (emergency repair diskette)
A rescue disk or a startup disk, created during or after installation using RDISK.EXE

ESD
Electrostatic discharge, an electrical shock caused when two objects (you and the PC) of uneven charge make contact. Electricity flows from high voltage to low voltage so, if you are carrying a build-up of static electricity, you can give your PC a shock.

Exposure to risk
An estimate of how likely it is that an event will take place. The estimation is based on a number of factors. Insurance companies, for example, estimate how exposed to risk a person or organisation is when they calculate premiums.

Feasibility study
An investigation when trying to resolve a problem within a given system. The feasibility

study provides a stepped approach to collecting, analysing and reporting systems information.

Fibre optic technology
A light beam travels down a thin glass tube with a refractive coating at the speed of light, does not suffer from noise or other disadvantages of the cheaper cabling options.

File transfer protocol (FTP)
The set of rules used for exchanging files over the Internet.

Firewall
Hardware or software that filters incoming internet traffic. It prevents applications from accessing data on the PC it protects.

Flash BIOS
A rewritable type of BIOS you can change using special software, rather than having to change the whole chip. However, it is vulnerable to attack by a virus which can also overwrite the chip, making it unusable.

Flash
An application used to develop animations and interactive applications for websites.

Fragmentation
When files have to split up into sections and are saved in separate locations on the disk because there is no contiguous space available that is big enough to hold the entire file.

Functionality
The general quality of something being useful, useable or having a use. Specifically in ICT it is a feature or element within an operating system which improves the use of the application, device or operating system.

Gantt chart
A project plan which displays a time line, with tasks allocated a time span, to show how the interaction of tasks can affect the completion date of the project.

Global gateway
A gateway that can be accessed, at any time, anywhere (providing you have the necessary hardware and software) and by anyone. It is an international network of information and resources that is not restricted by geographical or cultural boundaries.

GUI (graphical user interface)
What the user sees in order to be able to use the computer system.

Hacking
Unauthorised access to a computer system.

HCI (human computer interface)

Hit counter
Records the number of visitors to a website to date.

Hotlink
Text or an image which, when clicked on, takes you to another page within a website or to another website altogether.

Hotspot
Similar to a button except the link is text which normally appears in a different colour, to distinguish it from other text that is not a hotspot.

HTML
The abbreviation for hypertext markup language, which is the code used to create all web pages.

IDE (integrated drive electronics)
The current standard technology for transmitting data from a hard drive which can support up to two drives per cable. Most computers have two IDE cables so they can support four devices.

Intellectual property (IP)
A person or organisation's ideas, inventions or 'creativity' (for example, the work of writers or artists).

Intellectual property rights (IPR)
Protect a person or orgaisation's 'property' under the Copyright, Designs and Patents Act.

IRQ (interrupt request)
Peripheral devices gain attention from the CPU by placing a flag to show they need processing time; the CPU notices the flag, deals with the IRQ and then resets the flag.

ISDN
Integrated digital subscriber network.

ISP (internet service provider)
Includes btinternet, demon and yahoo.

Iterative
An approach which involves revisiting a design as many times as necessary to produce the desired effect.

JPG
(Pronounced jay-peg) the term for the image format devised by the Joint Photographic Engineers Group. (The E was dropped for historical operating system reasons.)

Jumper
A small switch used to configure the hardware.

Kernel
The innermost area of the system.

Keylogger
Software which records every keystroke made.

Knowledge worker
Anyone whose job involves the development or use of knowledge, including anyone in ICT fields.

LAN
Local area network.

Landline
A fixed telephone connection at home or work, a connection that travels over terrestrial circuits.

LDAP (lightweight directory access protocol)
Technology not (yet) as widely used as OLE. It allows a system to share common 'directory' information with other systems, independent of its technology.

Linux
A free and open source operating system developed by Linus Torvald that can be installed on your computer. Because of the open source movement, there are many versions of Linux available and they all interact with each other.

Master
The storage device which is in control; in a computer the hard drive used to start the operating system.

Mbps (megabits per second)
A measurement which indicates how quickly data is transferred on a normal Ethernet network system.

Metatag
A piece of code used to instruct the browser as to how to display the content of the web page.

Modelling tools and techniques
Tools which can, for example, help perform advanced calculations, add rules to given sets of data, forecast and predict values for a given point in time.

Modem
An abbreviation for modulation/demodulation; a device which converts the signal that the computer creates into one that can be sent along the telephone line (this is called modulation), and then back again at the receiving end (called demodulation).

Motherboard
The body of the computer, supporting all the components that run in the computer system.

MPEG (pronounced em-peg)
The digital moving image format developed by the Movie Players Engineers Group.

Multimedia
Computer technology which integrates images (video, graphics, text) and sound to produce interactive and entertaining products.

Multi-user games
Designed to be played by a number of users, usually in real-time.

OLE (object linking and embedding)
A technology that enables, for example, a Microsoft Excel® spreadsheet to be imported into a Microsoft Word® document, or for a Word® document to be recognised by other applications. OLE is a standard feature of Microsoft applications. Other operating systems use OpenDoc to enable applications to 'see' each other.

One-to-many relationship
A relationship that can exist between records on two different tables. The 'one' end of the relationship table has individual records which can be related to many records on the other table, for example, in a doctors' surgery database each doctor on the Doctor table can be related to many patients on a Patient table.

Open source software
Software which anyone is free to use or adapt, on the understanding that they do not re-sell.

PDF (portable data format)
Documents in PDF format always retain their pagination and layout when you download them. This is not true of other formats, such as the .doc files created in Microsoft Word.

Personal data
Information about living, identifiable individuals. Personal data does not have to be particularly sensitive information and can be as little as name and address.

PnP (Plug 'n' Play)
A configuration standard which allows the BIOS and your operating system to recognise and automatically configure a peripheral as soon as you plug it into your computer.

Power surge (or power spike)
Can be caused by an anomaly in the electrical supply grid, for example a lightning strike. This results in a very large voltage for a very short period of time.

Private sector organisations
Organisations owned by individuals or shareholders. They range from self-employed people to large multinational corporations such as Ford, Sony and Tesco.

Prototype
An initial version of a website, showing the navigational links that are proposed and the overall design (use of colour and images to create a theme).

PDSU (power supply unit)
Provides electrical energy to the computer from the power source at the socket. It converts the incoming supply into one suited to each component, and also houses a fan used to cool the PC.

Public sector organisations
Organisations funded by the public through taxes providing services to the public. They are controlled by the government and are accountable to them and the public. Examples include schools, libraries, local councils, the police and the armed forces.

RAM
Random access memory; a type of memory that is lost when power is removed – also called volatile memory.

Real time
Refers to events that take place more or less immediately.

Registry key
A unique reference to a device or driver in the operating system.

Relational database
A database which uses a system of tables and links (called relationships) to store and manage large quantities of data.

Resolution
The number of pixels (image units) per image; the resolution offered by an average digital camera is 1024 × 768.

Rollover
An area on screen which, when the cursor is moved across it, something happens, like the area changes colour.

RS323
An American standard; the European equivalent is V.24. An RS323 port is a serial port.

RSI
An injury caused by a repetitive action in a limited range of movement (for example playing tennis or the guitar). In terms of computer use it can arise from poor typing technique and posture when typing.

RTF (rich text format)
A text format available for transfer of data independent of the system.

Screen grab (or screen shot)
An image created from the screen display.

Scrolling marquee
A message that moves across the screen, repeatedly.

SCSI (small computer serial interface)
A standard device used for higher speed systems, such as file and web servers. Some systems can support up to 15 hard drives.

SCSI (small computer systems interface)
An expansion card, installed on the motherboard, allows the PC to support more peripheral devices than the IDE channel. The SCSI then copes with the systems resources such as IRQs for the devices that are attached in this way.

Secure connection
A connection used to protect information (such as credit card numbers and personal information) as it is transmitted from the customer to a website. The data sent is encrypted so no one else can read it.

Semi-conductor
The electrically sensitive material used to make a central processor.

Serial ATA (or SATA)
Serial advanced technology attachment, a high speed technology now used for the transfer of hard drive data. Most newer, larger hard drives use SATA connections.

Service level agreement
A legal agreement that defines response time; level and method of technical support; whether you will get new for old, in the case of a fault; and the terms and duration of any repair warranty.

Service pack
An update to an operating system.

Shareware
Software that can be obtained and downloaded free of charge.

Shopping basket
An icon which serves the same purpose as a real shopping basket, i.e. you place the items you intend to buy inside the shopping basket and then, when you have finished shopping, you take it to the checkout to pay for your purchases.

SIMM (single in-line memory module)
A mini-expansion board. The edge connector has either 30 or 72 pins, and its capacity ranges from 1Mb to 16Mb.

Single user games
Games played individually.

Slave
Any additional storage device which resides in your computer system.

SME (small to medium business enterprise)
An organisation with a workforce of 5–25 employees.

Source code
The original programming code used in the development of a web page or an application.

Spam
Unsolicited or junk mail, which could carry a virus in an attachment.

Spyware
The name often given to advertising-supported software. This is normally used by shareware authors to get information on your computer habits and activities.

SRAM (static RAM)
A memory type in which the transistors do not need frequent refreshing to 'remember' the data it holds.

Stock control
The methods an organisation uses to track and record the stock it has.

Stock
The goods that a company has in storage which, in the case of a commercial organisation, is waiting to be sold.

Storyboard
A panel or a series of panels of rough sketches that can outline a sequence of events or activities in a story, normally associated with a plot or film production. A storyboard can be used in the initial stages of developing an e-book where rough ideas and designs can be sketched to form the basis of each page.

Structure chart
A geographical representation of the overall structure of a product, similar to an online site map.

Style sheet
Default styles used to format a document. They can be altered to a preferred style.

Surge suppressor
Protects a PC against problems with the external supply by taking the hit from any power surge.

Synchronise
Two devices ensure that they are holding the same common data.

Systems model
A model which defines the start of the system (its evolution), the mechanics of the system (how it works, etc.) and the completion of the system (what happens next).

Template
A master document that can be used again and again which contains basic information that can be changed for the particular circumstances.

TFT (thin film transistor)
The technology used in new flat panel and notebook computer displays.

Toolbar
The list of icons you will see at the top, bottom, left or possibly right hand side of any application.

Transaction
An agreement to provide goods or services in exchange for payment.

Transactional website
A site where visitors can complete some kind of transaction, such as ordering and paying for goods or services. Other types include sites provided by banks, where customers can check their account balance, transfer money and pay bills.

Transistor
A micro-circuit switch, like the one which turns on your light, but at a considerably smaller level.

Trojan
A virus which infiltrates a PC by pretending to be a file or program that would normally be found on a PC. It is designed to allow others unauthorised access to your computer. It can cause problems and, because it is 'disguised', it can be difficult to track down.

UHF (ultra high frequency)
A method of describing the way the television signal is carried.

URL (uniform resource locator)
Often the address of a file that holds the HTML code for a web page. However, it can also specify a file holding an image, or some other resource needed within a website such as a sound track or video sequence.

Utility
A useful program, often supplied with a PC, or you may purchase it from a specialised vendor. Utilities do things like rid the memory of unneeded temporary files and tidy up how files are stored within the hard disk.

Vector
A numerical store of information about an image, it holds only two coordinates for each shape. Although vectors take very little time to download, you need additional software to view them (e.g. Flash Player).

Video conferencing
A communication technique using audio and video links to allow remote groups of people to have a 'virtual' meeting.

Virtual Learning Environment (VLE)
An environment that has been set-up to promote online learning based on flexibility and choice.

Virus
A file which will inflict some form of damage to your computer system; like a medical virus, it can self-replicate, infiltrating your computer from another infected computer.

Visual basic extension
Data that can be linked to a variety of other computer, software and operating systems.

W3C
A forum for information, commerce, communication and collective understanding. It develops material – such as specifications, guidelines, software and tools – to lead the Web to its full potential.

WAN
Wide area network.

Web authoring software
Software which helps the user create web pages and links to other sites, and enables the transfer of the website to the WWW.

Web server
A computer which runs software that responds to requests to display web pages.

Webmaster
The person who looks after a website on a day-to-day basis. He or she will make changes to the website – or supervise others who do the work – to improve the site and to fix any problems that arise.

Wireless
A radio-based communication system which can reach up to 100 metres.

Worm
A malicious program that can move itself from computer to computer via e-mail or the internet.

Y-splitter
A connector that allows you to run two cables together so that they only need one power source.

ZIF (zero insertion force)
A no-strain connector for a processor on a motherboard.

Zip
A program which uses compression techniques to reduce the size of a file, without losing any data within the file.

INDEX

acknowledging sources   xv, 35
Advertising Standards Authority   64
Amazon.com   43, 45–6, 54, 55, 62
animation   xvii, 112
archiving information   17–18
ASCII files   xi
assessment   xvii–xviii
   digital economy   38–9
   information age   2–3
   knowledge worker   83–4
auction sites   16, 22, 45, 54
audience, e-book   30
automatic processing   9

back-office processes   56–60
backups   ix, x
banking   40
   impact of ICT   21
   online   16, 20, 54
bar codes   20, 40, 41
bar graphs   106
bitmap format   xi
blogs   12, 15
Bluetooth technology   6
box, text   79
broadband   3, 5
browser software   32–3
businesses and Internet   7, 17

call centres   42
CD handling and storing   xvii
cell referencing   104
Chart Wizard   106
charts   27, 96, 112
chat services   5, 6, 12, 14, 19
chip and pin cards   45
civil rights   21, 22

codes of practice   xv–xvi
collaborative working   7, 17
commercial companies   39
communication in information age   19
   Internet   12–15
competitions   61
Computer Misuse Act (1990)   10, 21
conditional formatting   103
confidential files   ix, xi
confidentialit   xv, xvi
   of e-mails   13
consumer protection legislation   63–4
contents, table of   xvii, xviii, 30
cookies   61–2
copying existing work   xv–xvi, 35
copyright   xv, 7, 10–11
   software   10
Copyright, Designs and Patents Act   10–11
credit cards   40, 42, 44, 45, 52, 58–9
crime and Internet   21–2
CSV files   69–70, 72
customer relations   42
customers   7
   authentication   57–8
   awareness   63
   expectations   46
   registration   60
   tracking actions of   57
customising
   settings   xii
   toolbars   xii

data capture and processing   40–1
data controller   8
Data Protection Act (1998)   8–9, 21, 63
   rights of individuals   9
data subjects   8

database
    combining data   74
    field types and formats   67
    filtering records   74–5
    identifying trends   77–9
    importing given data   69–72
    queries   72–5
    reports   75–7
    selecting fields and sorting data   72–4
    transactional websites   66–7
deadlines   xiii
debit cards   40, 42, 44, 45, 52
decision-making   20, 84, 85, 86–101
    assessment of situation   88–9
    evaluation of information   93–4
    factors to consider   94–5
    investigation and fact-finding   90–3
    sources of information   89–94
despatch and delivery   59
diagrams   79, 80
digital divide   7, 11, 23–6
    BT report   24, 26
    economic factors   23
    and fear of technology   23, 24
    geographical factors   23, 24
    lack of motivation, knowledge and skills   23, 24
    social factors   23, 24
    technological factors   23
digital economy   37–81
    ICT skills required   79
digital technologies   3, 5, 6
digital television   6
Directgov website   16
directories   ix, x
disabled users   24
Distance Selling Regulations   63
distribution of goods   42
domain name   43–4
dot com bubble   44
downloaded information   17–18
drawing tools   79, 80
DVD (digital versatile disk)   xvii, 6

e-books   26–31, 45
    content   26, 27
    creating   29–31
    development issues   30

ease of use   26, 28
evaluation   28, 30–1
fitness for purpose   26, 27
format and fonts   27
images   36
language and style   26, 27
multimedia in   26, 27–8, 36
navigation   26, 28, 30
presentation of   26–8
storyboard   29
structure and layout   26, 27
template   30
types of compilers   29–30
e-commerce   15
education, effect of ICT   19–20
education resources online   8, 16, 20
electronic data interchange (EDI)   41
e-mail   x, 5, 7, 12–13, 41
    advantages   13
    attachments   19, 41
    disadvantage   13
employment, impact of ICT   7, 11, 21
encryption   13, 64, 65–6
entertainment and Internet   14, 17, 20
e-portfolio   xvii–xviii
    authenticating   xvii, xviii
    collecting information   xvii
    compatibility   xvii, xviii
    ease of use   xviii
    file formats   xvii
    structuring   xvii
e-voting   16
extranets   7

Favorites   32–3
Federation Against Software Theft (FAST)   11
file formats   xvii, 36
file management   ix–xii
file transfer protocol (FTP)   5
filenames   ix, x
filters   103–4
firewalls   64, 66
flash movie (.swf)   xi, xvii
flow diagrams   79, 80
flybmi website   49, 50, 51, 52, 53, 54
folders   ix, x
fonts, e-books   27
footnotes   xv

formal presentations   110
formal writing   27
formatting   ix, x
   cells   101–2, 103
   file xvii,   36
   slides   111
   spreadsheet data   101–3
   word processing   108
formula auditing   105
formulae and functions   104
free speech   21, 22
Freedom of Information Act   9

gaming   14, 17
.gif format   xi
global gateway   12
government departments online   16
grammar check   xiii, xiv
graphs   27, 96, 106–7

hackers   10, 47
hard disk loaders   11
health and safety   xvi–xvii
Heinemann website   49, 50, 51, 52, 53, 54
help, using sources of   xii–xiii
History   32
home, working from   7
HTML compilers   29
HTML in e-portfolio   xvii
Human Computer Interface (HCI)   55
hyperlinks   xvii, xviii, 34
hypertext   26

images in e-books   36
Import Text Wizard   70–2
industrial companies   39
informal presentations   110
informal writing   27
information about customers   62–3
information age   1–36
   assessment objectives   2–3
   benefits and opportunities   4
   ICT skills   32–5
   issues and challenges   7
   life in   19–23
   opportunities   6–7

Information Commissioner   9–10
information sharing   6
inserting files   108
intellectual property rights   10
interaction with others   7
Internet   3–5, 7
   and businesses   17
   communication   12–15
   lack of access to   11
   methods of access   3–4
   online information   17–18
   as research tool   32–5
   as unregulated   21
internet piracy   11
interviews   90–1
intranets   7
ISP (Internet Service Provider)   4
iTunes website   48–9

job losses   11
.jpg format   xi, xvii
just-in-time manufacturing   43

knowledge worker   8, 11, 82–113

landline   3, 4
language
   of e-book   30
   of spell check   xiv
laptops   6, 7
layouts, document   109
legislation   xv–xvi, 22
   and copyright   10–11
leisure planning online   20
licences, software   11
lifelong learners   7–8
lighting and safe working   xvi–xvii
line graphs   107
logical operators   33
loyalty schemes   20, 61

macros xii
marketing goods and services   42, 43
media handling and storing   xvi, xvii
messaging services   12, 14, 19, 22
mobile phones   5, 6, 7, 11
mobile technologies   7

modelling   97–101
   considering alternatives   99
   evaluation   100
   justifying decision   99
   reporting to others   99–100
monitor, correct positioning   xvi
MP3 format   48
multimedia   3, 5
   in e-books   26, 27–8, 36
music industry   48–9

Napster   48, 49
navigation
   e-books   26, 28, 30
   of websites   33–4
networks
   mobile phone   5, 6
   virus protection   xi
   wireless   5, 6
newsgroups   5, 6, 12, 14–15

observation   91–2
one-to-many relationship   69
online conferencing   12, 15
online services   12–19
online store, setting up   43–4
ordering online   20
organisations
   capturing and processing data   40–1
   categorising   39–40
   conducting transactions   41–2
   information needs   39–43
   presenting and exchanging information   41
organising work   x
ownership of software   10

password   xi, 58
payments, online   15, 20
   processing   58–9
PDAs   6, 7, 22
PDF compilers   29–30
.pdf format   xi, xvii
peer group pressure   23
personal data   9
personal effectiveness   xii–xiii
phishing   64
pictures   27, 112
pie charts   106
plagiarism   xv–xvi, 35

planning your work   xiii
.png format   xi, xvii
pornographic sites   21–2
PowerPoint   xvii, 110, 111–12
presentations   6, 106–7
   checking   112
   importing data   112
   inserting pictures   112
   producing   110–13
   software   110–12, 113
   styles of delivery   110
print preview   xiii, xiv
privacy rights   7, 8–10
private sector organisations   39
problem-solving   84–5
proofreading   xiii, xiv, 30
public sector organisations   39, 40
purchase histories   61

quality assurance   xiii–xv
questionnaires   91, 92

read only formats   xi
readme files   ix, xi–xii
real-time information   14
removable storage media   17
reports
   database   75–7
   producing   80
research using Internet   32–5
   acknowledging sources   35
   quality of material   34
   search engines   32, 33
   template   35
rich text format   xi
rights of data subjects   9
risk assessment and electronic payments   64–5
routing of e-mails   13

safe working   xvi–xvii
Sale of Goods Act   64
sales information   61
saving work   ix, x
scatter graph   107
screen shots   80
search engines   32, 33
secure connection   58, 59
secure sockets layer (SSL) encryption   65

security   47, 65
   of e-mails   13
   electronic transactions   54, 64–5, 66
sensitive information   ix, xi
service companies   40
services, online   17–18
settings, customising   xii
shareware   62
shopping basket   49, 52, 57, 58, 61
shopping online   7, 20, 43
   back-office processes   56–60
   benefits   45–6
   customer base   45
   disadvantages   46–7
   extension of product range   45–6
   real-time stock information   46
   response times   46
   set-up and running costs   45
   twenty-four hour opening   46
shortcuts, creating   xii
slides   110, 111–12
social effect of ICT   22
social exclusion and ICT   24, 26
software piracy   10–11
spam   13
spell check   xiii–xiv, 80
spreadsheets   95–7
   analysing data   103–4
   checking and validating   104–5
   entering and editing data   101
   formatting data   101–3
   functions   97
   modelling   97–101
   modifying   107
   sort function   104
spy ware   62–3
standard ways of working   ix–xviii
   authenticating work   xiii, xiv–xv, xvii
   file management   ix–xii
   legislation and codes of practice   xv–xvi
   personal effectiveness   xii–iii
   quality assurance   xiii–xv
   safe working   xvi–xvii
   seeking views of others   xiv
stock control   20, 39, 59, 61, 66
storyboard   29
SUMIF   97
surveys   61
systems model   84–5

tables   27, 67
technical information   ix
template   6
   document   xi, xii
   e-books   30
   Internet research   35
.tif format   xi
toolbars, customising   xii
tools and techniques   xii
training   8, 11
transactional websites   44–5, 47, 49–55
   attracting customers   54–5
   customer registration   52, 53
   purpose and structure   49–52
transactions   39, 41–2
transference   10

user friendly software   24
user groups   32
user IDs   65
utility companies   40

validation rules   68
vector graphic animation format   xi
video conferencing   17
virtual   43
virtual communities   7
Virtual Learning Environment (VLE)   16, 17
viruses   ix, xi, 10, 64, 66

WAP technologies   22
warehouse   59, 61
web browsing   5
web server   56
websites   42
   design of   55
   navigation   33–4
   see also transactional websites
wireless technologies   3, 5–6
   networks (WLAN)   5, 6
wizards   70–2, 76, 106, 111
word processing   108–10
   checking documents   109–10
   importing data   108
working
   flexible locations   7
   standard ways of   ix–xviii
   styles   19
workstations   19

x-drive   17